THE LEGAL GUIDE
TO COMPUTER
SOFTWARE PROTECTION:
A Practical Handbook
on Copyrights, Trademarks,
Publishing, and Trade Secrets

THE LEGAL GUIDE
TO COMPUTER
SOFTWARE PROTECTION:
A Practical Handbook
on Copyrights, Trademarks,
Publishing, and Trade Secrets

Thorne D. Harris III
Attorney at Law

Prentice-Hall, Inc.
Business and Professional Division

Englewood Cliffs, New Jersey

Prentice-Hall International, Inc., *London*
Prentice-Hall of Australia, Pty. Ltd., *Sydney*
Prentice-Hall Canada Inc., *Toronto*
Prentice-Hall of India Private Ltd., *New Delhi*
Prentice-Hall of Japan, Inc., *Tokyo*
Prentice-Hall of Southeast Asia Pte. Ltd., *Singapore*
Whitehall Books, Ltd., *Wellington, New Zealand*
Editora Prentice-Hall do Brasil Ltda., *Rio de Janeiro*

© 1985 by

PRENTICE-HALL, INC.

Englewood Cliffs, N.J.

This publication is designed to provide accurate and authoritative information in regard to the subject matter covered. It is sold with the understanding that the publisher is not engaged in rendering legal, accounting, or other professional service. If legal or other expert assistance is required, the services of a competent professional person should be sought.

. . . From the Declaration of Principles jointly adopted by a Committee of the American Bar Association and a Committee of Publishers and Associations.

First Printing September 1984

Editor: George E. Parker

Library of Congress Cataloging in Publication Data

Harris, Thorne D.
   The legal guide to computer software protection.

   Includes index.
   1. Copyright—Computer programs—United States.
2. Computer programs—Patents. 3. Computer contracts—
United States. I. Title.
KF3024.C6H37   1985   346.7304′82   84-9874
                        347.306482

ISBN 0-13-528373-6

ISBN 0-13-528365-5 {PBK}

Printed in the United States of America

Dedication

To my wife, Mary, without whom this book could not have been written and nothing would be worthwhile.

About the Author

Thorne D. Harris III is a practicing attorney in New Orleans, Louisiana. He attended the Louisiana State University School of Law, from which, after participating on the Louisiana Law Review, he graduated "Order of the Coif" and 15th in the largest class in the school's history. He is a member of the following sections of the American Bar Association: Science and Technology; Patent, Copyright, and Trademark; Corporate; and Litigation. In connection with his ABA activities, Mr. Harris has served on committees on Copyright and New Technology, Video Games and Software Technology, Proprietary Rights in Software, Software Licensing Practices, Contracting for Computers, and Litigation Support Systems. Mr. Harris is also an active member of the Louisiana and New Orleans Bar Associations and a member of the sections on Litigation, Mineral Law, Insurance, Business, and Antitrust of the Louisiana Bar Association.

In his ten years of practice he has represented OEMs, software houses, and programmers, both in litigation and in business. He is the owner of an IBM PC/XT and an Apple II and is an accomplished programmer in his own right. His "Legal Bits" column in *Nibble* magazine, a publication catering to Apple computer owners for which Mr. Harris is a Contributing Editor, regularly covers legal topics of interest to the computer community. In addition to his computer-related activities, he is a past editor of the "New Developments in the Law" section of the *Louisiana Bar Journal*, and a member of the American and Louisiana Trial Lawyers Associations and the Volunteer Lawyers for the Arts.

A Word from the Author

This book provides a practical guide to solving numerous problems involving computers and the law. It is designed for computer users, programmers, software publishers, businesspeople, and nonspecialist attorneys. In short, anyone involved with computers may benefit from this book. While sufficient discussion of the reasoning and background behind today's legal requirements is included to give the reader a solid footing upon which to base his or her knowledge, the concentration is on practical step-by-step outlines and applications. Complete instructions and guidelines for obtaining, completing, and registering copyrights in computer programs, visual displays, and animation are included. Additionally, sample forms, contracts, and correspondence—as well as case histories—set forth specific examples of applications and problems facing those in the computer industry.

For the individual, the user, the programmer, and the hobbyist, this book will serve as a guide to understanding the legal rights and obligations that arise in the course of writing and using computer programs. It will also enable nonattorneys, in noncomplex situations, to protect their rights themselves, without needing professional help, by guiding them through the copyright process and explaining exactly what protection is available. In more complex matters, the individual programmer or publisher will be better able to understand and discuss the legal problems involved with an attorney when familiar with the information provided herein. Tips on choosing a computer lawyer are also included. Additionally, contracts for publishing, using, writing, and leasing software are explained to give the reader a better understanding of the reciprocal obligations involved.

For the nonspecialist attorney, this book will provide insight and can be used as a guide and checklist for advising clients in this new and exciting field of law. Practical examples and sample forms are used extensively to provide a concrete working base. Additionally, references to lead cases and other major authorities facilitate any necessary further research.

There are now more than 2 million microcomputer owners in America, and that number is expected to double within the next year. Estimates have put revenues in the personal computer industry alone at more than $5 billion by 1985, and analysts tell us that anyone who doesn't know how to operate a microcomputer in the next few years will be considered illiterate. There are also many billions of dollars spent each year in other computer-related industries and areas. Clearly, the age of a computer in every home and office is upon us, and an understanding of the basic legal concepts necessary to function in such a computer society is needed. And so is a practical guide to computer law.

Virtually every owner and other user of a personal computer, such as the IBM, Apple, or TRS-80, at some time feels that he or she has written, or could write, a program that he or she will want to copyright or otherwise protect so he or she can sell or market it. Unfortunately, most people have no idea of how to proceed and either abandon the thought immediately or are intimidated because they believe they must engage an attorney and incur substantial expenses. While there are sound reasons for obtaining legal counsel in some instances, it is also possible to secure a copyright quickly and inexpensively without an attorney. I once received a call from a programmer who, after reading one of my articles on how to copyright computer software, was amazed that he could obtain his own copyright for his program for $10.00, rather than the $150.00 his lawyer wanted to charge. This is not to say that such a fee was unreasonable. You pay for the attorney's time and the security of using a professional. Many individuals feel safer with an attorney, or do not have the time or inclination to attempt such projects themselves. Certainly an attorney is called for in those situations. If a specific legal question is involved, again, professional help is required. For those who would rather do it themselves, however, this book will show them how.

Once a program has been protected, the possibility of venturing into the software business is presented. A recent estimate put the number of software development companies in the United States alone at almost 15,000. Most of these started with little or no capital or experience. Some even lost important rights to their programs by not fully understanding the copyright implications of their actions. This book will help entrepreneurs and their advisors to avoid these pitfalls. Established companies and individuals in the computer and data processing fields will also benefit from a better understanding of the legal ramifications of their contracts and actions. With more companies entering the industry every day, and with business relations becoming more complex and requiring specialized knowledge of new laws and interpretations, it will become even more important to understand this new technology and how the legal system will adapt to it.

Whether you have just written your first program on your home computer and would like to protect your rights or you are a computer professional or advisor to one and need a handy reference work with simple, straightforward, and practical information, this book should be of great interest and significant value.

Thorne D. Harris III

How to Use This Book

This book is designed as a handbook for the software programmer, publisher, advisor, and attorney. As such, it eschews in-depth legal analysis in favor of practical suggestions. Also, because of the numerous subjects covered, in some cases only a brief treatment is allowed. However, sufficient information has been given to alert the reader to the common pitfalls and practical problems involved.

The book is divided into five major sections. Part I contains introductory material designed to familiarize the reader with the terminology and underlying concepts that are necessary to an understanding of the later subject matter. There is a brief treatment of "computerese" for the nontechnical reader and a similar discussion of the law for the nonattorney.

Part II focuses on copyright. Since this is the easiest and most often used form of legal protection of computer software, it is given prominence herein. Besides the rights and obligations involved, concrete examples and completed forms are given to assist the reader in completing his or her own applications for registration.

In Part III, some of the other methods of legal protection are considered. Specifically, trademarks, trade names, trade secrets, and patents are covered. Again, with respect to trademarks and trade names, example applications are provided.

Part IV takes up the consideration of some of the more common contracts with which the reader might become involved. Specific examples and samples of actual contracts are provided. In this way, the reader can see the law in action.

Finally, in Part V, some additional items are covered that do not fit conveniently into the other categories. For example, a chapter on how to choose a computer lawyer should be very helpful. This section also gives the author an opportunity to express some of his personal views.

It is hoped that this organization will facilitate the use of the book. Although unnecessary duplication has been avoided so that each chapter may stand on its own, certain information is occasionaly repeated where necessary to complete the idea under consideration. In this way, at a later date the reader can simply turn to the chapter that relates to the particular problem at hand and find an answer or at least some guidance.

Contents

PART THREE. OTHER FORMS OF PROTECTION

PART FOUR. CONTRACTS AND AGREEMENTS

PART FIVE. MISCELLANEOUS

APPENDICES

Part One

COMPUTERS AND INTELLECTUAL PROPERTY

1. Anatomy of a Computer— Some Basic Terminology

REFRESHER COURSE

While the programmers who are reading this book to learn the law undoubtedly do not need a refresher course in computer terminology, most attorneys—not to mention more casual computer users—are not so fortunate as to have an innate understanding of binary numbers or hexadecimal notation. Consequently, here are a few words to familiarize those who need it with some of the basic terms involved in the study of computers and the law.

Let's demystify the computer. Although it is certainly not necessary to know all of the inner workings of a computer to be able to choose a machine intelligently for the home or office or to write a program, some understanding of what a computer does and how it works is essential. As Samuel Johnson said, "You don't have to know how to build a table to know when one is crooked." Well, it is still important to know what the table is supposed to do! Also, an understanding of the terminology is essential to an understanding of why certain forms of protection are or are not available and the consequences resulting from their use.

THE OBEDIENT IDIOT

Many computer professionals have referred to their machines as obedient idiots. This phrase underscores the fact that the computer can do nothing on its own. A human being must first program it. But the first word of the phrase—

obedient—is also very important. The computer excels at doing repetitious steps or calculations over and over again without complaint and, assuming the program is correct, without errors caused by fatigue or boredom. And it does these things very fast! This ability to do repetitive acts with great speed accounts for the initial use of digital computers as number crunchers. Mathematical and arithmetical formulas, which would take months or years to evaluate by hand, can be processed in minutes or hours by computers. But that's all they can do.

HARDWARE

The physical machine itself is generally referred to as the *hardware*. This is to distinguish it from the *software,* or programs that are required to make the computer useful. Software will be discussed in more detail below.

The hardware is usually comprised of a keyboard, CRT screen (cathode ray tube, or television), the internal electronics of each, and at least one enclosure to house all of this equipment. Other hardware items include printers, disk drives, monitors, plotters, telephone modems, cables, and many other *peripherals* (components connected to but not an original part of the computer). These systems come in all shapes and sizes. Some are all-in-one units, while others are made up of many different components connected by cables, much like a stereo system. There are also portable computers smaller than a briefcase.

CPU—CENTRAL PROCESSING UNIT

The *central processing unit (CPU)*, which can be thought of as the brain of the machine, is usually contained on an *integrated circuit (IC) chip*. These silicon marvels, containing the equivalent of thousands of transistors and other components, are also referred to as *chips*. However, there are other types of chips as well, such as those that store computer memory or information and chips that modify or amplify a signal. There are also chips designed for special purposes, such as the regulation of the fuel supply on many new cars or the control of heating or industrial processes.

The CPU, however, is usually a general-purpose, frequently patented and copyrighted device, which is not susceptible to change by the user. It directs all of the other parts of the computer and acts as the central point for all activities. Without the CPU, there would be no computer as we know it.

MEMORY—ROM AND RAM

In addition to a processor, for a computer to be versatile and not dedicated to just one function, it must have some form of *memory* to store the information it will use and manipulate. The memory comes in two basic types: *volatile* memory, which is generally transient and used in the actual computing process because it can be accessed very rapidly (and is lost if there is a power outage during the process), and *nonvolatile* or *permanent* memory.

The permanent memory installed in and always accessible to the computer is usually referred to as *ROM* or "read only memory." This memory is available to the computer for fast, immediate use but cannot be changed by the user or by other programs. It frequently also contains a highly proprietary operating system, or *language*, which the computer uses to interface with the programmer. In personal computers, the ROM may be in ICs or in plug-in cartridges. Its main features are that it cannot be modified and it is not lost when the power is turned off.

These attributes distinguish ROM from *RAM,* or "random access memory," which is also available *on-line* (within the computer immediately), but which can be accessed and modified by user programs. This is where the computer program is stored as it is entered. In this way, fast access to the RAM in the computer provides a way to compute and manipulate data, which can then be stored safely *off-line* (outside the computer proper) on a disk. Don't become overly concerned about the terminology here, as this will become much clearer when each individual topic is covered. Later I will discuss the problems involved in conceptualizing and placing in the legal system software, algorithms, and other computer concepts.

BINARY NOTATION—ON AND OFF

In reality, a computer is just a large group of switches. It can only tell the difference between ON and OFF, sometimes referred to as SET and CLEARED by programmers. Since ON and OFF can also be represented numerically by 1 and 0, the computer is considered to be *digital*. Further, since all it can "see" is 1 and 0, the *binary* number system is used. In binary there are only two symbols—1 and 0—rather than the 10 used in our more familiar base ten system. Instead of each place in a number representing a multiple of 10 ($1111 = 1000 [10^3] + 100 [10^2] + 10[10^1] + 1[10^0]$), the places denote multiples of 2 ($1111 = 8[2^3] + 4[2^2] + 2[2^1] + 1 [2^0] = 15_{\text{BASE 10}}$). Consequently, the binary representation of the number 4, which is "100," is simply a matter of one switch being ON followed by two OFF switches.[1] For example:

BASE 10	BASE 2
1	1
2	10
3	11
4	100
5	101

While this may seem cumbersome and not very useful initially, when you can put a large number of switches, which are either ON or OFF, side by side, and then look at a group as a whole, you can see that a number of different combinations are possible. If you assign each combination a unique value—such as a letter of the alphabet, a word, or an instruction to do something—you can easily see that the switches can be used to represent and accomplish almost anything. Sets of instructions that accomplish certain functions are called *algorithms* and are the building blocks for computer programs. This software will be discussed in more detail below.

SOFTWARE

The programs that actually enable this mass of switches to accomplish anything useful are referred to as *software*. This distinguishes it from the hardware, which is the actual equipment, the "box."

Software can take many forms, from the operating system, which must interact with other programs, to an arcade game. The basic concept is the same. Certain electronic impulses are recorded which are then translated by the microprocessor into particular actions. By combining these in a certain fashion, the desired result is obtained.

Operating Systems

One group of software is comprised of *operating systems*. These are generally fundamental programs that interface directly with the processor and allow other programs to be run. As will be seen later, these programs are nearest to the machine itself. Examples of operating systems include the various disk operating systems (DOS) for the many different personal computers and others, and the basic monitor routines also found in those systems.

Operating systems are usually written in machine language. That is, the code is directly understandable to the microprocessor. Unfortunately, the more understandable the program is to the computer, the less comprehensible it usually is to humans. Generally, machine code is nothing but a string of hexadecimal or binary numbers. Therefore, higher level languages were developed to make life easier for the programmer. Without an operating system, however, other higher level languages could not operate.

Higher Level Languages

There are many languages in which programs may be written. Most home computers, for instance, support a version of BASIC, which stands for Beginner's All-purpose Instruction Code. Other languages include COBOL, FORTRAN, APL, LOGO, and Pascal.

Since these languages cannot be understood directly by the computer, programs written in them must first be translated into the machine's native tongue. This is accomplished either by an *interpreter* program, which does the conversion as the program runs, or by *compiling* the higher level language into machine code. Although it is not necessary to have a detailed understanding of these functions to protect software legally, some knowledge is important in comprehending why certain legal problems might exist. For example, translating from one language to another, or compiling, may be very important because of an increase in the speed of a program that no longer needs an interpreter. The protection of such conversion rights will be discussed later.

Application Programs

The last broad category of software is comprised of *application programs.* These are the programs, usually written in one of the higher level languages, that perform a specific function. They actually make the computer do something as far as the nonprofessional is concerned. They range from complex accounting programs to arcade games and frequently are broadly distributed. They are also the programs that most require legal protection by copyright, trade secret, and other means. Consequently, they will be the focus of most of the discussions in this book.

NOTES

1. Another commonly used computer numbering system is hexadecimal (HEX) or base 16, in which there are 16 elements, the familiar 0–9, plus A–F.

2. Defining Intellectual Property and the Rights to It

A DIFFICULT CONCEPT

Intellectual property can be a somewhat difficult concept to pin down precisely. This type of property is intangible and incorporeal. As such, it differs from a car, a table, a chair, or a book, all of which are personal property. Likewise, intellectual property does not refer to the family homestead, land investments, or other so-called real property. It does relate to secrets, names, ideas, or at least the expression of those ideas, and a number of other similar concepts.

The creator of an intellectual work, whether it is a book, an invention, a play, a musical composition, or a secret process, has certain rights to that work. Naturally, he or she can keep it a secret and secure all of the benefits for himself or herself. The author can also decide to give the work to the world . . . and receive little or nothing additional for his or her creation. The law of intellectual property attempts to forge a middle road whereby the public at large can obtain some benefit from new ideas while at the same time providing for just compensation to the creator of the work.

EXPRESSIONS AND IDEAS

Since intellectual property, such as copyright, is intangible and incorporeal, it exists apart from the physical form in which it is embodied. However, it is nonetheless inextricably related to that form. For example, an idea for a book cannot be copyrighted, although the book can be. Once the words are reduced to writing, they are susceptible of protection. However, it is not the physical book itself that is covered. Selling the book certainly does not sell the right to the text, the intellectual property rights. Although a sale of the book will transfer ownership of that piece of personal property, it is insufficient to transfer the ownership of the work itself. You only buy the book.

This close relationship between ideas and the expression of those ideas is central to an understanding of the means the law has provided to protect invention and innovation. Generally speaking, ideas are not susceptible of protection until they are incorporated into some work. In the abstract, an idea is, in a sense, in the public domain. Anyone can think of it, repeat it, and use it. However, the expression or use of the idea in literature, science, industry, and almost any other human creation is usually protectable. Therefore, while the idea for a book on the antebellum South can't be copyrighted, one would be ill advised to attempt to reproduce *Gone with the Wind* as one's own work. Similarly, no computer programmer can corner the market on a sorting function, but particular programs and applications can be copyrighted.

HISTORICAL SETTING

Despite the difficulty of defining just what the right is, the law has recognized that there should be some way to prevent others from capitalizing on the work and brilliance of an inventor or author. That some form of legal protection is appropriate has been recognized for centuries. Perhaps the earliest form of copyright protection grew out of certain grants to printers under the king's prerogative in England. These grants were enforced through Star Chamber decrees as early as the sixteenth and seventeenth centuries. Then came licensing statutes that prohibited printing unless a book was first registered. However, it seems that these early laws were designed more as a means of censoring printed material than as a way to grant the authors protection from unauthorized copying. In any event, by 1709, the Statute of Anne was enacted, which granted authors exclusive rights for up to two consecutive 14-year terms. This actually forms the basis of our modern statutes.

Nor were the Colonies silent on this issue. In 1672, Massachusetts adopted an order that provided that no printer could produce more copies than were agreed to and paid for by the owner without the owner's consent. When the Constitution was written, Section 8, paragraph 8, provided that Congress shall have the power:

> To promote the progress of science and useful arts by securing for limited times to authors and inventors the exclusive rights to their respective writings and discoveries.

From these few words we have derived a considerable body of patent and copyright law. These rules, together with the vagaries of trademark, unfair competition, and numerous state laws, make it very difficult for the nonprofessional to understand fully the intricacies and problems involved in protecting intellectual property. These words do, however, give the foundation upon which much legal reasoning is based, and also contain some very important philosophical insights into the whole protection concept.

PURPOSES OF PROTECTION

The Supreme Court restated the philosophy behind the modern intellectual property protection laws of the United States in 1954 as follows:

> The economic philosophy behind the clause empowering Congress to grant patents and copyrights is the conviction that encouragement of individual effort by personal gain is the best way to advance public welfare through the talents of authors and inventors in "Science and Useful Arts."[1]

Protection must serve the dual purpose of allowing the author or inventor to gain from the work while at the same time promoting the arts and sciences. While it is true that providing such exclusive rights should encourage prospective authors and inventors, it is also true that exclusive rights can be used to hold back progress. That is why the exclusive grant is for a limited time.

A time limit ensures, at least in theory, that a work will eventually become the property of all the people and thereby prevents an individual from withholding something that might better humanity indefinitely for personal gain. For example, there is the old story about the man who invented a means for changing water into high-grade gasoline for pennies, but the oil companies supposedly bought the process. If such a process was patented, after the appropriate time periods had elapsed it would be available to the general public. Also, the process would have to be described in detail to obtain a patent. In these ways, the advance of science and technology is encouraged while still giving the creator of a work some exclusive rights.

EXAMPLES

Perhaps an easier way to understand what intellectual property can be is to give a few illustrations. The most obvious, perhaps, is a book. Yet, as we have seen, it is the story or the writing that is the intellectual property and not the physical book. The same is true for music and inventions. But there are other categories. For example, a celebrity has been held to have certain property rights to his or her name and can sell those rights to others. The rights to the name, symbol, slogan, and card for the old television program "Have Gun Will Travel" has been the subject of litigation. (Unfortunately for the plaintiff claiming to have the exclusive rights to these items, the court found that no attempt to copyright or otherwise protect them resulted in the loss of any rights he might have had.) There are, of course, numerous other examples that could be listed. However, this book will relate these various concepts to the specific subject of computer programs—that is, how to legally protect your computer software.

NOTES

1. *Mazer* v. *Stein,* 347 U.S. 201, 219 (1954).

3. The Different Methods of Protecting Intellectual Property

VARIOUS MEANS OF PROTECTION

Although each method will be covered separately and related specifically to computer software later in the book, a brief description of the major systems that have been used to protect such intellectual property rights is helpful as a backdrop against which to study the specific problems of the computer industry. Indeed, these same procedures have been tried with respect to software, as well as other forms of intellectual property, with varying degrees of success. There are also certain rights to privacy that might be invoked with respect to certain aspects of an individual's life, but these are beyond the scope of this book.

It is also important to understand that the different categories represent attempts to formulate more or less coherent rules regarding the basic concept that a creator of a work should be able to obtain and benefit from the fruits of his or her labor. Since all of these rules stem from such an amorphous beginning and were developed historically over a long period of time, there will be some overlap, and some aspects of the rules will seem less than logical in today's environment.

The primary forms of protection we will be dealing with are:

1. Copyrights
2. Patents
3. Trade Secrets
4. Trade Names and Trademarks
5. Unfair Competition

COPYRIGHTS

Generally, any original work of authorship fixed in a tangible form may be the subject of a valid copyright. This would, of course, include books, poems, songs, and all other forms of writings. Copyright also covers art, photographs, graphics and drawings, and most anything else that can be reduced to writing or to a picture. Almost any original expression that can be reduced to writing or to some other tangible form can be copyrighted. There is no need for it to constitute a new discovery or for it to be novel. It just must be original. The importance of these distinctive terms will become clearer in later chapters on copyright.

Although the copyright exists by virtue of creation of the work, registration with the Copyright Office adds important rights and grants procedural advantages. Once obtained, a copyright is valid until 50 years after the author's death. During that time, no one may legally reproduce, copy, and, in the case of those works so susceptible, perform the work without paying the owner of the copyright a royalty or otherwise obtaining permission. However, as will be discussed more fully, only actual copying is prohibited, and there are no restrictions upon someone else who independently creates the same work or one very similar. Nor is there any protection for the ideas, as opposed to the expressions, contained in the work.

The procedures for registering a copyright claim with the Register of Copyrights in Washington, D.C., are also fairly simple and straightforward. A completed application, two copies of the work, and $10.00 are the primary requirements. A more detailed discussion and a step-by-step outline of the procedure with examples of completed forms will be given later. Because of its cost-effectiveness and the ease of securing and maintaining it, copyright protection is frequently the method of choice.

PATENTS

The granting of a U.S. Letters Patent results in the holder possessing the exclusive right to make, use, license, and sell the substance of an invention for 17 years. As such, the protection afforded is considerable. Patent, unlike copyright, protects the idea embodied in the invention as well as the particular expression of that idea. Independent creation of the same device or work is no defense to patent infringement, since a valid patent is, in essence, a limited, legally granted monopoly.

However, the cost of obtaining a patent and the procedures necessary for such render this form of protection far more difficult to obtain than others, such as copyright. For example, although it is possible for an individual to pursue his or her own patent application, a patent attorney is generally required. The work this specialist will do includes a search of prior art, since only a new and original invention can be the subject of a valid patent, and a detailed description of what the invention is and how it accomplishes its purpose and functions. If these descriptions are not sufficiently detailed and technical, the Patent Office will surely reject the claim. Even after all of the necessary work to obtain a patent is completed, it may take a year or more for the Patent Office to issue a patent. Considering these factors, and knowing that there is still some question about the patentability of computer software, this method of protection is seldom attempted for a computer program.

TRADE SECRETS

A trade secret is just that—a secret used in a trade. It is sensitive, confidential information not generally known, which is treated confidentially. The very nature of trade secrets demonstrates this method's strengths and weaknesses. Only so long as something is kept secret can it be considered a trade secret. Once it becomes common knowledge, such protection is lost. Therefore, a great deal of effort and expense must usually be invested in a trade secret.

However, trade secrets may be comprised of ideas, works, inventions, formulas, and almost anything of commercial value. Also, because of its nature, there is no specified time period for which a work, formula, or product may be considered a trade secret. Unlike copyright and patent, as long as appropriate means are taken to ensure the confidentiality of the secret, it may exist as such indefinitely, and anyone stealing or misappropriating the secret may be prosecuted. An example of such a trade secret is the formula for Coca Cola. It is certainly a well-guarded secret, although it has been around for a long time. Just as certainly, the company considers it one of its greatest trade secrets and would undoubtedly prosecute anyone who misappropriated it.

TRADE NAMES AND TRADEMARKS

Trade names and trademarks are the particular names, logos, or marks that are associated with a particular company. They are created by actual use of the mark and can be lost by nonuse. Although trademarks may be registered nationally, trade names may not be, and somewhat different rules apply. (See Chapter 18.)

The rules regarding the use of these names and marks arise out of the common law regarding unfair competition. Generally, protection is afforded only in the limited areas, both geographically and in terms of product, in which the marks have been used, and, as with copyright, registration offers certain procedural advantages. Once a product becomes known, trademark protection adds to the bundle of rights the author or seller has in that it inhibits others from capitalizing on his or her good name. There are good reasons to use this method of protection in conjunction with others.

UNFAIR COMPETITION

The law of unfair competition is derived from the notion that no one should be allowed to capitalize on the work of another person in such a manner as to mislead the public. As such, it forbids "pawning off" one product as another, and prohibits misleading and deceptive practices that would tend to make the public think a product was something it was not. This doctrine is almost always invoked in conjunction with one of the other forms of protection discussed above as a way to fill in the gaps of any unauthorized activity. Because of this overlapping, a separate section on unfair competition is not included later in this book.

INCOMPATIBILITY AND OVERLAP OF DIFFERENT METHODS

Sometimes one form of protection is incompatible with another. For example, to obtain a patent, full disclosure of the process, the prior art, and everything necessary for another professional in that particular field to understand how to use the invention must be disclosed. After such a complete disclosure, trade secret protection would certainly be unavailable. This is more than an academic consideration, since experts do not always agree on a particular form of protection.

Similarly, certain works may be susceptible of both copyright and patent protection. For example, under the new Copyright Act, sculpture may be the subject of a valid copyright. Certain sculptural works might also be patentable. In these cases, the law allows dual protection. This result may also obtain in connection with certain computer firmware on ROM chips, as will be discussed in greater detail later.

Furthermore, in certain situations a combination of protective devices is warranted. For example, it might be decided that the most effective means of protecting a video game is to copyright the video display, thus prohibiting others from making a game with a similar display. However, the author may want to keep his or her programming tricks secret and therefore not register the program with the Copyright Office. Or the author might copyright the object code while utilizing trade secret protection for the source code. In any event, a proper copyright notice would still be necessary. Later chapters will contain a more complete discussion of the pros and cons of each method and their interrelationships.

4. How Computer Programs Fit into the Picture

LEGALLY DEFINING A COMPUTER PROGRAM

Before a work can be classified as coming within the reach of a certain law, we must first have a working definition. This in itself has presented certain problems in connection with computer software. Indeed, the rather elusive term *software* as used by those in the computer industry may refer to several distinct conditions or elements of a total package.

Each of these different elements is loosely referred to as the program or software and they are in fact related. However, they are not identical, and each has its own peculiarities that sometimes affect its treatment under the law of intellectual property. Indeed, trying to explain just what constitutes software to someone without any computer experience can be quite a challenge.

A Set of Instructions

Many would define a program as a set of instructions that directs a particular computer to perform a specific task. While it is accurate, this definition does not really resolve the confusion. Although we know that a program of some sort is necessary for any computer to be of use, it is sometimes difficult to determine where the program begins and ends and where it is at a particular time.

This is because of the multiple use this word receives. For example, there are a number of ways such a set of instructions can be depicted. These include a symbolic representation in a higher level language (words on paper), flow charts and diagrams (also on paper), the actual electronic activities that occur when the program is in the computer, and the disk or tape on which the program is recorded.

Listings

The written representation on paper of the set of instructions is often referred to as the program. This might be a listing of a program written in BASIC or the source code listing of an assembly or machine language program. Certainly these representations are the most meaningful to human beings, and without them the life of a programmer would be much more difficult. It is also easy to argue that such a written expression is a written work of authorship, which, as will be shown, has significance in the area of copyright law. Such a listing of a simple BASIC program routine might be as follows:

Simple Program Routine

```
10 IF A = B THEN GOTO 40
20 PRINT "NO"
30 END
40 PRINT "YES"
50 END
```

Although the simple routine above is certainly understandable to any programmer with even a smattering of BASIC, unless that representation is moved from the paper and translated into something a computer can understand, such as by typing the program into RAM, the written program cannot be understood by the computer. Since the computer can't pick up a book and read it, before this program can accomplish anything the additional step of somehow getting it into the computer is required.

Flow Charts

There might also be flow charts, schematics, and other representations of the program that would enable an experienced programmer to enter the program into a computer and use it but would be useless without this further human intervention. For example, a flow chart of the program described above might look like Figure 4–1.

Program Descriptions

Additionally, a description of the program, which is sufficiently detailed for a programmer to write the code from it, might be considered to be the

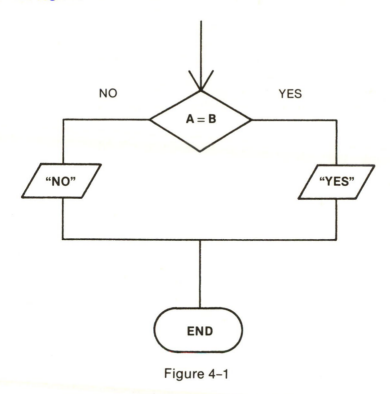

Figure 4-1

program. An example for our sample program routine could be expressed as the following:

Description

1. Test to see if A is equal to B.
2. If so, skip to line 40 and print "YES."
3. If not, print "NO."
4. Stop.

Electronic Impulses

It is readily seen that these three methods of describing this simple program are very different, yet it is the same program. Nonetheless, none of these versions is capable of making the computer do anything, at least not until it is keyed into the memory of the machine.

Once this program is entered into a computer's memory, it exists in another form. Specifically, the program is now a collection of electronic impulses in the RAM memory of the computer, which can actually direct the computer to perform some action (assuming the program works and was typed in correctly). Unfortunately, it is difficult to diagram such. Actually, at this point the program has been converted into a series of electric charges located within certain sections of individual integrated circuit (IC) computer memory chips. Certainly, this is completely different from the written representations of the same program on paper, and yet it is frequently referred to as the same program or software.

Storage Media

At this point the program may be saved on a disk, tape, or some other form of permanent storage device. Now the program is a collection of magnetic impulses arranged in a particular order, more than likely on a magnetic medium. Most software is sold or leased in this form, and the recorded program is far more useful than a written representation.

Although in this form the computer will not be able to carry out the function or purpose of the program, if the medium is in a format that can be read by the computer system, then the program can be loaded into the computer's memory without the necessity of reentering the program from the keyboard. Therefore, this loading makes the saved program much closer to the program in memory than the written representation of the program. Nonetheless, they are not the same.

VARIOUS SUGGESTIONS

In order to deal more effectively with these various situations, there have been several proposals to amend the copyright laws specifically to provide for these distinctions. For example, proposed Resolution CS-2 of the American Bar Association Section of Patent, Trademark, and Copyright Law, which was not acted upon in 1982, would have amended Section 101 of the 1976 Copyright Act, deleting the present definition of *computer program* and substituting the following:

> A "computer program" means a set of instructions capable, when incorporated in a machine-readable medium, of causing a machine having information processing capabilities to indicate, perform, or achieve a particular function, task, or result.

> A "program description" means a complete procedural representation in verbal, schematic, or other form, in sufficient detail to determine a set of instructions constituting a corresponding computer program.

> "Supporting material" means any material, other than a computer program or a program description, created for aiding the understanding or application of a computer program; for example, problem descriptions and instructions.

"Computer software" means any or several of the literary works referred to in the definitions of "computer program," "program description," and "supporting material."

Under this proposal, a copyright of the software would consist of many parts, each of which would be protected. Consequently, each of the different representations of our sample program would be covered. However, it is easy to see that there may be some legitimate confusion about where program description ends and computer program begins, and it is questionable whether a flow chart diagram should be treated as a copy of a program listing. Similarly, different standards may, of necessity, apply to the different aspects of the software.

There have also been several other proposals for revamping the law with respect to protection of computer software. These include recommendations from the World Intellectual Property Organization (WIPO), the Association of Data Processing Service Organizations (ADAPSO), the National Commission on New Technology Uses of Copyrighted Works (CONTU), IBM Corp., and others. However, none of these proposals has gained enough support to become law. Consequently, rather than adopt an artificial definition, which is not accepted by the courts, to avoid these problems, the discussion in this book will reflect the practical problems inherent in the rather amorphous terminology actually in use.

OTHER PROBLEMS

There is another fundamental reason why the law and lawyers have so much difficulty with computers and computer programs. Attorneys and judges tend to be conservative by nature, and the law is slow to evolve. This is often good, since it provides a certain amount of needed stability in any lasting legal system. However, when a fast-moving and rapidly expanding new field like computers must be dealt with, it causes problems. Furthermore, the law is generally not susceptible of the mathematical precision of computers, and the legal profession is sometimes intimidated by this advanced technology. This creates even more problems. (See Chapter 26.)

Nonetheless, in an effort to afford as much protection as possible while also protecting the public as a whole, the legal system has done a fairly admirable job in keeping up with technology. Traditional doctrines developed in simpler times have been adapted to modern science with varying degrees of success. We now turn to a discussion of some of the means devised to protect this very important, albeit new, technology.

Part Two

COPYRIGHT

5. Copyright—An Overview

WHAT'S THAT REM?

Almost everyone has seen a copyright notice, such as:

Copyright © 1984 by
Thorne D. Harris III.
All rights reserved.

These notices appear opposite the title pages of books, on greeting cards, in catalogs, on photographs, and even in newspaper articles. Additionally, many BASIC computer programs, when they can be listed, will contain a similar notice in a REM statement. (A REM statement in a BASIC program allows the programmer to include remarks, without affecting the program.) A typical notice might appear as follows:

```
 5 REM DOOM VALLEY
10 REM Copyright (c) 1984
15 REM SUPERIOR SOFTWARE Inc.
20 REM All rights reserved.
```

QUESTIONS

Aside from realizing that such a notice means that the reader is restricted from copying the work and distributing copies, most nonprofessionals do not fully understand exactly what is protected and the extent of that protection. Are copies for friends allowed if no one is charged? Can copies be made for home use?

What about multiple copies for work? Although the answers to these questions may affect many users, most people do not have a clear understanding of what is permitted and what is not.

Similarly, although almost all computer programmers are aware that copyright protection is available, they do not know what is involved or what can be copyrighted. Most are in the dark regarding such basic questions as: When does copyright protection start? What happens if a modification is made? What kind of notice requirements are needed? When do you have to file for registration? Is there any protection if you don't file?

Nonetheless, many attempt to place some form of notice, such as that noted above, on their work. As will be seen, depending on the program and the notice, this may result in some protection, even without registration. However, with a better understanding of the rights involved, more complete protection can be obtained.

COPYRIGHT ACT

The copyright laws of the United States are set out in Title 17 of the United States Code, beginning at Section 101 (17 U.S.C. 101, *et seq.*). Additionally, numerous rules and regulations regarding the procedures and interpretations of the Copyright Office in Washington, D.C., are published in the *Federal Register*. These promulgations are codified in Title 37 of the Code of Federal Regulations (37 CFR). For those with a desire to receive the latest information, the Copyright Office regularly distributes on request its publications relating to new procedures and rules. Additionally, a number of informative pamphlets and circulars can be obtained from the Copyright Office by writing:

Register of Copyrights
Copyright Office
Library of Congress
Washington, D.C. 20559

AVAILABILITY OF COPYRIGHT

Although recent cases indicate that patent protection may be available to computer programs when used in conjunction with a "machine" or "invention"[1] (the criteria involved and protection afforded will be discussed in later chapters), the most often used form of registered protection is copyright. But only certain types of works are susceptible of copyright protection, so it is important to know what can be the subject of a copyright in order to make an informed decision about how to protect a computer program.

Indeed, there are still many controversies surrounding the copyright protection afforded computer programs, with some still claiming that certain computer programs, such as operating systems embodied in ROM, are not susceptible of copyright. However, today the majority favor the copyright of software. The Copyright Office has accepted applications for copyright registration of computer software since 1964. Additionally, since 1980, the Copyright Act has specifically included a reference to computer programs.

STATUTORY COPYRIGHT BEFORE 1978

Copyright protection has traditionally been of two types: statutory and common law. Statutory copyright was the protection granted pursuant to the Copyright Act and the regulations and cases decided thereunder. Under the Copyright Act of 1909, statutory protection was not available until a work was published. Note that, contrary to what the lay person may understand, the words *published* and *publication,* when used in conjunction with copyrights, are terms of art that actually mean "distributed to the public." Consequently, no publication by a publisher as used in the common parlance is necessary. Photocopying a work and giving it to several people can, under certain circumstances, constitute publication under the copyright laws. Because a number of important rights result from such publication, and the loss of important rights can occur if publication occurs without appropriate notice, when a work was first published was a very important consideration under the law before the amendments that took effect in 1978.

COMMON LAW COPYRIGHT BEFORE 1978

Under the old law, the other category of work that might enjoy some protection was unpublished works. This was referred to as common law copyright because it was not pursuant to the congressional act that protection was afforded but rather the common law of the various states. This means that the protection could be different in each state and from state to state for the same work. Usually there were few state statutes covering the subject, so reliance was on case law. Again, once the work was published the federal statutory rules superseded the common law protection.

THE NEW ACT

The Copyright Act of 1976, which became effective on January 1, 1978, subsumed the earlier common law copyright law as well as the statutory protection. Both published and unpublished works created after January 1, 1978, are covered by its provisions. However, the 1909 act still applies to works, including computer programs, produced before 1978. Consequently, questions in that time period relating to unpublished works will still be controlled by the common law. However, since statutory copyright now comes into existence upon creation of the work rather than upon publication, the distinction between unpublished and published works in many respects is effectively abolished for works created after January 1, 1978.

Although many of the earlier inconsistent treatment of published and unpublished works has been abolished, and the newer rules are less harsh with respect to notice requirements and publication, it is still possible to lose important rights by not taking the necessary precautions. Additionally, as mentioned, there are still some significant questions regarding coverage, and it is often felt that a combination of copyright and other forms of protection is needed to gain the maximum protection for your work.

EASE OF OBTAINING COPYRIGHT PROTECTION

One of the most attractive features of copyright is the ease with which registration can be accomplished. Chapters 16 and 17 will take you step by step through the process of completing and submitting the appropriate applications for several different kinds of copyright registration. Such registration, while not necessary to establish the basic right, grants significant advantages, including the right to sue in federal court and for statutory damages. If registration is not timely, some of these rights may be lost. Consequently, there is little excuse for not properly registering at least certain aspects of a program. Later chapters will show you exactly how and when to do this.

NOTES

1. *Diamond* v. *Diehr,* 101 S.Ct. 1048 (1981).

6. What Can Be Copyrighted

Copyright protection is available, pursuant to Section 102 of the Copyright Act, for "original works of authorship fixed in any tangible medium of expression." The Copyright Office first announced that it would accept computer programs for registration in 1964. This was long before the 1980 amendment to the act which specifically mentioned computer programs. It was also before the new Copyright Act of 1976, so all of the distinctions between unpublished and published works were also necessary considerations in any evaluation of the methods for obtaining legal protection for computer software during this time period.

Since computer programs were not specifically provided for in the act, to be eligible for copyright protection the first consideration was to determine if software would fit the description of copyrightable matter. As noted, only matter meeting the definition in the act could be the subject of a valid copyright.

Certainly, it is clear that some work is involved, and if that work is original it would seem that the first criteria are met. However, the old law had some difficulty with machine-readable materials, and generally copyright registration was allowed only for those programs reduced to a form intelligible to humans. That is, computer programs were registered as original writings under Section 5(a), which covered "books, including composite and cyclopedic works, directories, gazetteers, and other compilations." Since the concept of writings had already been extended into such areas as photographs, sound recordings, and motion pictures, it was natural for the Copyright Office to accept the written expression of a computer program as a copyrightable writing.

The new act avoids this problem by granting protection to any work that is "fixed in any tangible medium of expression." By providing for the use of any tangible means of expression, the law attempts to anticipate new technologies without abandoning the basic requirement that the work be somehow fixed as an expression, as opposed to an intangible or fleeting thing. A floppy disk would certainly appear to qualify as a tangible medium, and the Copyright Office has in the past accepted deposits of such, although the present rule requires a listing of the program. However, even after the 1980 amendments, which specifically dealt with computer programs, it is still probable that an independent ground exists for registering software under the writing concept.

MACHINE-READABLE WORKS

One problem that is frequently alluded to refers to the case of *White–Smith Music Publishing Co.* v. *Apollo Co.*[1] This 1908 decision involved the issue of whether or not a pianola roll constituted an infringement of certain music for which a copyright had been obtained by registering the sheet music. In what has been a much criticized opinion, the Court held that the pianola roll was not a reproduction that was intelligible to human beings and consequently was not a violation of the copyright on the sheet music. The widespread copying by technologically advanced recording studios resulted eventually in the passage of the Sound Recordings Amendment to the Copyright Act in 1971, which specifically remedied this problem.

Nonetheless, the rationale of *White–Smith* must be taken into consideration when dealing with pre-1978 works, including computer software. Indeed, there are those who would say that it is still a good precedent, even after the new amendments affording protection to any expression fixed in tangible form. However, it would certainly appear that such a view would be a minority one today.

ROM AND OBJECT CODE

This unfortunately confusing state of affairs may explain one of the more distressing court decisions for the computer software industry. In a 1979 case involving JS&A Group, Inc., a large mail-order electronics concern, and Data Cash, a company that had developed a computer chess game, the court was asked to decide whether the direct copying of a ROM chip constituted a copyright violation under the 1909 Copyright Act.[2]

The trial court held that no copying had taken place because the ROM chip was a "mechanical embodiment" of a writing rather than a copy. The court went even further in suggesting that object code could never be the proper subject of a copyright because "in the object phase, the ROM, the computer program, is a mechanical tool or a machine part . . . engaged in the computer to become an essential part of the mechanical process, but it is not a 'copy' of the object program." While mechanical processes may sometimes be the subject of patent, machines may not be copyrighted.

This case provoked much public concern over whether copyright protection would ever be available to software and even made the cover of *"80" Microcomputing* in 1980, which depicted a federal judge with an oversized gavel smashing microcomputer disks and tapes.[3] Because it is the object code, or a similar binary coding as opposed to written statements in an understandable language, which is actually recorded on disks and tapes and in the computer's memory, the concern was quite understandable.

However, on appeal the lower court's rationale for the holding in *Data Cash* was changed. Although the ultimate decision was the same (no copyright protection), the court of appeal held that the reason for denying protection was that the Data Cash ROM bore no copyright notice. The formalities and necessity of notice, which are discussed more completely in later chapters, were not present on the chip, nor were they incorporated into the program in such a manner as to give proper notice to users. Under the law in effect at the time, publication without proper notice resulted in the loss of all copyright protection. (See Chapter 14 for a more complete discussion of this problem.) Consequently, the lower court's discussion regarding the absolute protectability of object code was completely side-stepped.

THE LAW TODAY

Although it seems well settled that computer programs may be a proper subject of copyright, there is still some uncertainty about the extent of that coverage. Perhaps a definitive answer will be forthcoming from the Supreme Court in the near future, but until then a certain amount of caution is required when approaching this subject.

For example, the plethora of Apple II copies and workalikes has spawned much litigation. In many instances, Apple Computer, Inc., was able to obtain a preliminary injunction that prohibited the other companies from selling their computers even while the case was still undecided. Additionally, Apple has been rather successful in stopping unauthorized importing of Apple II copies. These are frequently seized as they go through Customs.

However, in at least one case—Apple's suit against Franklin Computer Corporation, which will be discussed further in the next chapter—the trial court originally appeared once again to be concerned about ROMs and operating systems. An initial injunction was refused there, at least in part because of the doubts in the court's mind about the copyrightability of computer operating systems. However, on appeal the court held that ROM was susceptible of copyright protection and remanded the case back to the lower court for further proceedings in light of this ruling. Although the original decision involved only the denial of a request for a preliminary injunction, and other considerations such as the relative hardships of the parties may have predominated, the reversal of that decision tends to resolve the issue in favor of the copyrightability of ROMs.[4]

Indeed, in other cases decided at the same time as the original trial court decision, and later by other courts, it has been held that the copyrightability of computer programs, even in ROM, is "firmly established"[5] and that "there can be little doubt that computer programs are among the works of authorship covered by the Copyright Act."[6] Although there are appeals pending in some of these cases, it would seem that the majority view of granting copyright protection for all forms of computer programs will certainly prevail. The settlement of the *Apple* v. *Franklin* litigation after the decision of the Court of Appeals leaves that decision as the latest law on this subject.

NOTES

1. *White-Smith Music Publishing Co.* v. *Apollo Co.*, 209 U.S. 1 (1908).

2. *Data Cash Systems, Inc.,* v. *JS&A Group, Inc.,* 480 F.Supp. 1063 (N.D. Ill. 1979), *affirmed* 628 F.2d 1038 (7th Cir. 1980).

3. 10 *"80" Microcomputing* 54, 1980.

4. *Apple Computer, Inc.,* v. *Franklin Computer Corp.,* 714 F.2d 1240 (3rd Cir. 1983).

5. *Williams Electric, Inc.,* v. *Artic International, Inc.,* 685 F.2d 870 (3rd Cir. 1982).

6. *Tandy* v. *Personal Microcomputers, Inc.,* 524 F.Supp. 171 (N.D. Cal. 1981).

7. Expressions, Not Ideas, Are Copyrightable

COPYRIGHTABLE SUBJECT MATTER

Not everything you can think of is copyrightable. A very common but nonetheless mistaken belief is that ideas are protected by copyright. To the nonprofessional, the concept of "I thought of it first, so it's mine" might seem perfectly natural. However, the law attempts to be more precise in defining what can be protected and certainly is much narrower in that protection.

It is a longstanding tenet of copyright law that ideas are not protectable. That is, the abstract concept cannot be taken from the public, and further use of that idea cannot be prohibited. This prohibition is now contained in Section 102 of the Copyright Act:

> [I]n no case does copyright protection for an original work of authorship extend to any idea, procedure, process, system, method of operation, concept, principle, or discovery, regardless of the form in which it is described, explained, illustrated, or embodied in such work.

EXAMPLES

Although the idea may not be copyrightable, the particular expression of an idea is susceptible of copyright protection. Distinguishing between ideas or concepts and the expression of those ideas or concepts is sometimes difficult. A few examples might be helpful.

Mathematical formulas may not be the subject of copyright. Once discovered, the mathematician cannot preempt the use of the formula so that others will have to pay him or her royalties to use it. An author can, however, write a book or article describing the formula and its uses. Providing the work meets the other requirements of a copyrightable work, it would be forbidden for anyone else to copy any significant portion of the book or article without permission. This would not, however, prevent someone from writing another book on the subject, so long as the new work does not copy the original. A moment of reflection reveals the logic in this rule. Otherwise, how could there be different texts on the same subject?

Similarly, a sunset can't be copyrighted in a poem, nor can the concept of a board game, although a particular expression may. H. G. Wells certainly couldn't copyright the idea of space travel, but his stories were protected, and the many new ideas found in almost any field of literature are all subject to the same rules. So, too, are the technical writings describing new techniques and concepts. Note that if the discovery constitutes an invention it is possible that it might qualify for patent protection, which would also protect the underlying idea, although not purely abstract ones. This subject will be discussed in more detail later, but it is significant to note here that one of the primary differences between patent and copyright is that copyright protects works that teach and explain the art, while patent protection is available for that which is an essential element of the machine.[1] This concept has also recently caused a number of problems in dealing with ROMs and operating systems in computers.

COMPUTER PROGRAMS

The rule that only expressions and not ideas or formulas are susceptible of copyright protection is particularly vexing in connection with computer programs. While it seems clear that taken as a whole a program is a writing and should be accorded copyright protection even before the recent 1980 clarifications to the law, when the individual aspects of the program are considered in more detail the problem becomes much more difficult. This is in part because a computer algorithm has been likened to a mathematical formula, and, as has been seen, such formulas are not proper subjects of copyright.

In a simple example, it might be contended that, while the programmer's total effort may be copyrightable, thereby protecting the author from outright piracy, the sorting routines and other specific algorithms cannot be excluded from general use. This type of protection seems to be supported by the philosophy that copyright protection is designed to protect the original from duplication but does not grant a patent on the use of processes, machines, or methods. Similarly, the public good is furthered by allowing and encouraging the dissemination of new concepts and ideas without allowing people to capitalize unfairly on the legitimate work of others.

UNCOPYRIGHTABLE PROGRAM IDEAS

Practical examples of this situation abound in the computer field. The sorting example used above is a perfect illustration. It is almost impossible to pick up a computer programming text without seeing examples of the most commonly used sort routines. These are clearly formulas and are not susceptible of copyright. The same is true with respect to data matrices, file structure, and many other common ideas.

On the other hand, it is also generally conceded that if a programmer put these various elements together into a general-purpose data base system, copyrighted the source code (let's assume it is in BASIC for the sake of simplicity), and published it in a how-to book, an unauthorized copying of the program would constitute a copyright infringement. The author's expression of these ideas would be protected. The same considerations apply and the same type of confusion results as we move from a higher level language to a more primitive code.

CONVERSION OF A PROGRAM

As noted, there is little doubt that a computer program written in a high-level language such as BASIC is copyrightable. Assuming it meets the other requirements of originality and authorship and is fixed in a tangible medium of expression, and assuming further that any copy does not come under a special exception such as the "fair use doctrine," the program would be an expression of an idea, which is protectable. It is the feeling of some experts and courts, however, that as the method of obtaining the same actions or results as the original higher language program moves to the more primitive codes of lower level languages, object code, or ROM chips, copyright may not apply. At some point, they reason, the work ceases to be an expression and becomes more like an element of a machine, a formula, or a product of engineering. This was one of the reasons the district court in *Apple Computer, Inc.,* v. *Franklin Computer Corp.* originally refused to grant Apple a preliminary injunction prohibiting use by Franklin of Apple's operating system and certain ROMs pending the outcome of the case. (On appeal, the appellate court held that ROMs could be copyrighted and sent the case back for further consideration. The case was then settled.) An illustration is helpful in understanding the problems involved.

The BASIC Program

Let's start with a simple BASIC program. Although the example is not really original, and so would not stand up to an attack on its copyrightability, it is used for clarity and simplicity. The BASIC program is as follows:

```
5 HOME
10 PRINT "THIS IS A TEST"
```

The only functions accomplished by this program (for those nonprogrammers reading this) are, on the Apple II, to clear the screen and print the words "THIS IS A TEST" at the top of the screen. Although not much of a program, it is certainly an expression and a writing. One would be hard pressed to argue that, at least in its present form, it is an algorithm or mathematical formula. Therefore, if it were original and met the other copyright requirements, placement of the next line would ensure that copyright protection for this work would not be lost when it was published:

```
20 REM Copyright 1984 by
   Thorne D. Harris III
```

BASIC but Different

Now let's change this BASIC program a little to accomplish the same result, again ignoring questions of originality. The following BASIC program produces the same result:

```
5 CALL − 936
10 POKE 1024,212: POKE 1025,200: POKE
   1026,201: POKE 1027,211: POKE 1028,
   160: POKE 1029,201: POKE 1030,211
20 POKE 1031,160: POKE 1032, 193: POKE
   1033,160: POKE 1034,212: POKE 1035,
   197: POKE 1036,211: POKE 1037,212
```

Again, for nonprogrammers, a brief explanation: Line 5 CALLs (executes) a routine already present in the Apple monitor, which clears the screen. The POKEs literally place the characters on the screen by putting the ASCII code for each character in the memory locations associated with the first 14 screen positions.[2] The internal routines in the computer then convert these codes into the words "THIS IS A TEST."

Obviously, the two programs do not look at all alike, yet they produce exactly the same result. Has there been a copyright infringement? In this case, the answer is no. This is an example of reverse engineering, that is, studying the result of one work and creating another work that arrives at the same result without in any way copying or translating the original work. Reverse engineering will be covered in more detail in Chapter 10.

Assembly Language Version

The next step is to convert the BASIC program into an Assembly language listing. This is also commonly referred to as source code, because it is the source for the object code, which can be read by the monitor program or operating system already present in the computer. To clear the screen and produce our message at the top of the screen, an Assembly language routine such as the one the follows could be used:

```
              ORG      $300
COUT          EQU      $FDED
HOME          EQU      $FC58
              JSR      HOME
START         LDX      #$00
LOOP          LDA      DATA,X
              JSR      COUT
              INX
              CPX      #$0E
              BNE      LOOP
              LDA      #$8D
              JSR      COUT
EXIT          RTS
DATA          ASC      "THIS IS A TEST"
```

This version of the program bears only a vague resemblance to the original BASIC program, yet it was specifically derived from it. The BASIC program was converted line for line. There is authority for the position that a conversion from one computer language to another is a copyright violation to the same extent that an author's copyright is violated by translating a book written in English into French. Therefore, if a direct translation can be shown, a violation has probably occurred.

Remember, however, that reverse engineering is not illegal. Therefore, if a programmer works backward from the result, he or she can create an original work that, although it produces the same result, will not generally infringe on the copyright of the first original work. It will frequently be difficult to determine whether the copying occurred by translation or by reverse engineering when different computer languages are involved in the dispute. One probable exception, however, would be the use of compiler programs. Since these programs follow a specific set of rules for translations and simply convert a program from one language to another mechanically, it would seem possible to show such copying even if the original program was in BASIC and the copy was in Assembly.

Machine Code

The next step in the movement toward more primitive commands is a listing in machine code. This is a hexadecimal (hex) rendition of the binary code, which the microprocessor can actually understand. The above assembly language program would look something like this:

```
20 58 FC A2 00 BD 18 03
20 ED FD E8 E0 0E D0 F5
A9 8D 20 ED FD 60 D4 C8
C9 D3 A0 C9 D3 A0 C1 A0
D4 C5 D3 D4
```

Certainly, this rendering of our simple program looks less like a writing and more like a group of numbers or a formula. In fact, it is nothing but a list of hexadecimal numbers, which are contained in a series of memory locations in the computer. (Such a listing is frequently called a hex dump.) However, this list of numbers is simply a direct translation of the program into hex so that the processor will be able to act upon it faster. Actually, the assembly and hexadecimal listings above use certain routines already contained in the monitor, which simplifies coding. It also means that these machine language programs partake a little of the form of BASIC programs because they refer to other routines already present in the computer's ROM.

The hex listing itself was obtained by using another program, called an assembler. The assembler mechanically converts the source code into object code pursuant to a defined set of rules. Absolutely no additional creative effort or authorship was involved in going from the source code to the hex dump. Consequently, it would seem clear that a valid copyright on the source code should also protect the object code to the same extent. Unfortunately, things are not always what they seem.

The fact that object code appears so much like a formula has led some courts and commentators to claim that object code is not copyrightable. However, the majority opinion today seems to be that the translation of a higher level program into the lower level object code results in a predictable one-to-one relationship and thus is protectable by copyright. Until a legislative enactment specifically covering this point or a definitive decision by the Supreme Court, there will probably continue to be divided opinion. Nonetheless, the weight of authority clearly favors protection.

Binary Code

Carrying these steps further, even more difficulty occurs in attempting to apply the traditional copyright rationale to computer operations themselves and programs contained within ROM. The hexadecimal notations referred to above as object code are still not what the computer actually "sees." As discussed in Chapter 1, all a computer can understand at any given moment is ON and OFF. Therefore, for a more accurate rendition of how a microprocessor can act on the object code, it should be reduced to binary. Because of the amount of space a complete binary translation would require, only the first few numbers of our object code listing will be converted:

Hex	Binary
20	00010000
58	00101100
FC	11111100

What the computer responds to is a series of electronic impulses, which can be represented by the 1 and the 0 in the binary format. Such a list does not appear at all like what we started with.

ROM

The next and perhaps final step is burning the object code into a ROM chip. This is the part of the process with which the courts seem to have the most difficulty. Because a ROM is an electromechanical device in some respects, the binary code can be thought of as having been reduced to millions of tiny switches that are either ON or OFF. Indeed, earlier computers were actual collections of thousands upon thousands of switches, which were hard-wired into a particular pattern that would perform a particular function. To change the operation of the computer, the electromechanical switches had to be rewired. Later, the switches were designed so they could be changed more easily, until finally it was discovered that the switches could exist as electrical impulses within the computer's memory. This software could then be changed rather simply, and general-purpose computers came into being.

It is this switch analogy that has most perplexed the courts when dealing with the copyrightability of ROM. Certainly, no one would argue that a group of light switches connected with wire into a series is a copyrightable work of authorship. Under certain circumstances it might constitute a patentable machine, but not an expression subject to copyright. Similarly, it has been argued that the ROM is simply a very tiny machine containing millions of switches that are set in a particular pattern and therefore not susceptible of copyright protection. As noted previously, this was one of the grounds upon which Apple Computer, Inc. was originally denied a preliminary injunction that would have prohibited Franklin Computer Corporation from manufacturing computers that contained copies of Apple's ROM chips and operating system while the litigation between the companies was pending. Although this reasoning was overruled on appeal, the settlement of the case prevented the rendering of a definitive decision by the country's highest court on this issue.

NOTES

1. *Taylor Instrument Companies* v. *Fawley–Brost Co.,* 139 F.2d 98 (10th Cir. 1943); *Baker* v. *Seldon,* 101 U.S. 99 (1879).
2. ASCII is an acronym for American Standard Code for Information Interchange, which assigns a unique value from 0 to 127 to each of 128 numbers, letters, and special characters.

8. The Difference Between Copyright and Registration

REGISTRATION

Properly and legally speaking, the term *registration* refers to the actual filing of the appropriate forms and deposit copies with the Register of Copyrights in Washington, D.C. It also requires payment of a $10.00 filing fee. The necessary procedures to be followed, including a step-by-step outline and sample forms, are given in Chapters 16 and 17. Unfortunately, many people speak of "obtaining a copyright" when they are really referring to filing for registration. Attorneys are also guilty of this practice. While there may have been some justification for such terminology before 1978, today it is simply incorrect.

Registration does not confer a copyright. Although related, the two concepts are not synonymous. A copyright exists by virtue of the creation of an original work of authorship. It need not be published or registered in order to exist. However, both publication and registration can modify the rights afforded by the copyright, and, if improperly handled, publication can lead to the loss of all rights. Such improvident publication and its grave consequences will be discussed in Chapter 14.

PRE-1978 REGISTRATION

Before January 1, 1978, there was a distinct difference between published and unpublished works and when federal copyright law applied. At the creation

57

of the work, common law copyright was applicable. This common law was comprised of the jurisprudence of the individual state in which the author resided and, naturally, differed from state to state. Uniform protection under the 1909 act was afforded only to published works that were registered with the Copyright Office in Washington, D.C. At that point, statutory copyright, the laws embodied in the federal act, superseded and preempted state law.

Because federal law preempted state law with respect to all published works, the publication of a work effectively ended the common law copyright protection. However, federal protection was then afforded if and only if the precise requirements of the Copyright Act were met. If those requirements were not met, not only did the work not qualify for protection under the federal law, but, since it was published and state law had been preempted by federal law, the state common law protection was lost as well. The primary requirements necessary to avoid such an unpleasant state of affairs were proper registration and the inclusion of the appropriate copyright notice.

It should be noted that publication, as used in the field of copyright law, does not mean that a book or magazine publisher must accept and print the work. Perhaps the phrase that should be used is "distribution to the public." Any distribution, even if for free, to the public at large or to persons who are not within a select circle of friends, editors, or others who might qualify for the limited distribution exception is sufficient to constitute publication.

REGISTRATION UNDER THE 1976 COPYRIGHT ACT

The new Copyright Act was passed in 1976 but became effective on January 1, 1978. It applies to both published and unpublished works, thereby creating one national copyright law applicable to all works created on or after January 1, 1978. The author's copyright to a work exists by virtue of the creation of the work. No formal registration or any other act is required to create the copyright. Under common law copyright, the author's rights to an unpublished work existed until publication, when they were superseded by the federal law. Under the new act, the treatment of published and unpublished works is almost identical. The protection extends for the lifetime of the author plus 50 years, or 75 years after publication in the case of works for hire. (See Chapter 12 for a discussion of works for hire.)

Because the federal law now specifically provides that all state laws designed to provide the same kind of protection are superseded by the federal law, there are strong reasons to follow the Copyright Act and take full advantage of all of its provisions, unless there are compelling reasons for not doing so (such as protecting the secrecy of the algorithms). Otherwise, it is possible that the state law has been preempted and will not apply. This might leave the program completely unprotected.

Additionally, the act strongly encourages registration by making it a prerequisite to certain procedural and substantive benefits, such as an infringement suit in federal court and statutory damages.

ADVANTAGES OF REGISTRATION

The Copyright Act and the Copyright Office regulations thereunder set forth specific procedures and requirements involved in registering a copyrighted work. Although the copyright may exist without any filing, the act requires registration in almost all cases before an infringement action may be brought. Additionally, if registration has been refused, even though all appropriate forms, deposits, and payments have been made, the purported holder of the copyright may still bring an infringement action, although he or she must also notify the Copyright Office. Therefore, even if the Copyright Office refuses the work for any reason (such as a determination by the examiner that the subject matter is not copyrightable, which determination is not binding on a court), because of the attempt to register the work the procedural benefits will not be lost.

To further encourage registration of all copyrightable works, the act provides that statutory penalties, which may be granted regardless of actual provable loss, may not be given for infringement of nonregistered works. (See Chapter 15 for more information on infringement, penalties, and damages.) In fact, Section 412 of the act goes even further by eliminating the statutory penalties for violation of copyright to works that were not registered within three months of first publication. Although this is much more liberal than the earlier law, since the statutory penalties can be a deterrent to those who would deliberately pirate computer software, it is important to register the work within the first three months of publication.

WEIGHING OTHER CONSIDERATIONS

Although the steps for registration will be discussed in considerable detail in Chapters 16 and 17 of this book, it should be noted at this point that registration generally includes the delivery of a copy of the program to the Copyright Office. Since this will, of course, eliminate some secrecy, considerations regarding trade secrets, software or hardware protection schemes, and the like are also involved. (Some of the relative advantages and difficulties inherent in trade secrets as a form of protection are discussed in Chapter 20.) Nonetheless, the protections afforded by copyright can be significant, and a careful balancing of the necessity for secrecy, the possibility of loss of trade secrets, and the ease of obtaining the broad protection of copyright is required in any consideration of legally protecting computer software.

9. Rights of a Copyright Owner— An Overview

EXCLUSIVE RIGHTS

Subject to certain limitations, the copyright owner of any work has the exclusive rights to five important categories of actions regarding his or her creation. He or she may also sell or license these rights to another or make such other transfer of ownership as he or she deems appropriate. The copyright holder has exclusive rights to the following:

1. Public performance of the work
2. Public display of the work
3. Distribution of copies by sale, lease, rental, or lending
4. Reproduction of the work in copies
5. Preparation of derivative works

PERFORMANCE AND DISPLAY

The rights to performance and display have seldom been dealt with in connection with computer programs, being more commonly concerned with motion pictures, plays, and music. (An interesting digression is the fact that the song "Happy Birthday" is a copyrighted work, and for every use of it in a movie, television show, or otherwise, royalties must be paid. This also illustrates the virtual impossibility of policing copyright infringement on an individual basis.) Consequently, there is no real law on these aspects of software copyright.

It is possible, however, for these rights to be applicable to computer programs. An obvious example is the video arcade game. The performance and display rights on certain coin-operated games may well be some of the most important rights to the owner. Indeed, the rights to see the display and performance are being sold, and, judging by the number of quarters that have been spent on these machines, these are valuable rights. Similarly, if the audiovisual display is copyrighted as well as or in lieu of the actual program, these two rights of performance and display should be directly applicable. (Chapter 11 discusses the protection available for the display itself, and Chapter 17 explains how to register a copyright claim for one.)

DISTRIBUTION

The element of distribution is usually concerned with unauthorized copies and is treated in the same context. There seldom will be an authorized copy and at the same time an unauthorized distribution of such a consequence as to warrant litigation. However, it is possible for this to occur.

For example, permission might be given to a school to make numerous copies of a particular educational program for use in the classroom while at the same time prohibiting the school from selling or otherwise distributing the work outside the school environment. If, for instance, after the course was no longer being taught, an instructor, in an attempt to recoup some of the expenses the school incurred in teaching the computer course, then took the copies of the program down to the local computer store and offered to sell them, there would be an infringement of this aspect of copyright, even though the copies being distributed were authorized.

COPIES

The right to make or authorize copies is the seminal grant of power to the copyright owner. Copying of a protected work is also the most common form of infringement and the one with which the courts have dealt most frequently. Indeed, virtually all of the reported decisions involving the copyright of computer programs have concerned the copying of program code or audiovisual displays.

Because computer software is difficult to create but easy to copy, the legal right to prevent others from copying such software without permission is essential to any type of legal protection. Fortunately, as far as direct copying is concerned, there have been a number of reported cases in which the courts have held such to be an infringement of the author's copyright. Although there are still some unanswered questions with respect to ROM and object code, and the other requirements of a valid copyright must be met, it is generally settled that an unauthorized copy of a substantial part of a computer program is an actionable copyright violation.

DERIVATIVE WORKS

Derivative works are also covered by copyright. The act defines a derivative work as follows:

> A work based upon one or more preexisting works, such as a translation, musical arrangement, dramatization, fictionalization, motion picture version, sound recording, art reproduction, abridgment, condensation, or any other form in which a work may be recast, transformed, or adapted. A work consisting of editorial revisions, annotations, elaborations, or other modifications which, as a whole, represent an original work of authorship, is a "derivative work."

This definition is intentionally broad. However, while it was originally used in connection with written literary works such as novels, the concept can, with only a modicum of difficulty, be transferred to the realm of computer software. For example, the direct translation of a BASIC program into another programming language such as COBOL would seem to be clearly a derivative work. Likewise, the use of a compiler program or the direct translation of a high-level program into assembly or machine language seems to come within the rule. In each of these situations copying of the author's expression takes place. In fact, it is possible that these translations would not only be considered derivative works but could also be considered unauthorized copies. This is particularly true where a mechanical one-for-one translation occurs.

In one case, the use of a speed-up kit to modify the play in the game "Galaxian" was held to have resulted in the creation of a derivative work.[1] Unfortunately, what might be considered an illegal adaptation can also enter the realm of nonprotected actions, such as reverse engineering and the use of noncopyrightable ideas as opposed to protected expressions of those ideas. These subjects, which will be covered more completely in the next chapter, make life a little more difficult for the attorney attempting adequately to protect and advise his clients involved in the computer software field.

DURATION OF COPYRIGHT

The duration of a copyright under the new law is the author's life plus 50 years. This rule applies to works created on or after January 1, 1978, whether published or unpublished. If two or more authors collaborated on a work, the term extends for 50 years from the death of the last surviving author. If the work is anonymous or pseudonymous or if it was a work made for hire, the copyright endures for a term of 75 years from its first publication or 100 years from its creation, whichever comes first. Note that if the identity of at least one of the authors of an anonymous or pseudonymous work is made known by an appropriate filing, the normal 50-year rules apply.

PRE-1978 WORKS

Before the 1976 act, there were two separate schemes for the protection of copyrightable works. Unpublished works enjoyed a common law copyright, which could differ from state to state. This protection was generally without a time limit but ceased completely upon publication. Consequently, upon distribution to the public a work either entered the public domain or was copyrighted under the 1909 act. To obtain such a copyright required strict adherence to all of the formalities required by the copyright laws. The protection afforded under the 1909 act existed for a primary term of 28 years with the option to renew for an additional 28 years. Although the new act covers both published and unpublished works, provisions for works created before the effective date of the new act had to be made.

Copyright in a work created before January 1, 1978, which was neither placed in the public domain nor copyrighted under the earlier law, subsists for the same term as new works. To ensure no loss of preexisting rights, the act further provides that in no case shall the copyright expire before December 31, 2002, and if the work is published with the appropriate copyright notice affixed in a conspicuous place, the term shall not expire before December 31, 2027.

For works that already enjoyed statutory copyright protection on the effective date of the new law, there are specific provisions governing the original term and its subsequent renewal for various situations. The thrust of these rules, however, is to grant the original 28-year term and allow the renewal to extend the copyright by another 47 years. Therefore, the 75-year term applicable to anonymous and pseudonymous works is used, which is greater than the original 28-plus-28-year term under the old law.

Because of this extension of time for the duration of copyrights secured under the earlier law, certain additional rights to terminate transfers or licenses of copyrights executed before January 1, 1978, are given. The work must not have been done for hire, and the transfer or license must have been granted before the effective date of the new law. Additionally, special provisions are made with respect to deceased authors and the heirs who possess these additional rights. A complete discussion of all of the various rules relating to earlier works is beyond the scope of this book. Considering the rapid onset of obsolescence in the computer industry, it is unlikely that these rules will be used much in connection with the protection of computer software. However, should any of these problems ever become an issue, it is important to know that the treatment may be somewhat different from that of other works.

NOTES

1. *Midway Manufacturing* v. *Artic International, Inc.*, 211 U.S.P.Q 1152, 1982 Copyright Law Decisions, par. 16,883 (N.D. Ill. 1981).

10. Limitations on Copyright Protection

IDEAS ARE NOT PROTECTABLE

In Chapter 7, some of the difficulties encountered in determining what can be the subject of a valid copyright were discussed. Specifically, copyright protection, unlike trade secret protection (Chapter 20), extends only to the expression of an idea and not to the idea itself. Consequently, mathematical formulas, laws of nature, abstract concepts, and pure ideas cannot be copyrighted. Until your expression of that idea is reduced to some tangible form, whether it be on paper or on a floppy disk, no copyright can exist.

In the programming field, this means that things like sorting algorithms, basic program structures, and designs may be taken from your work without an infringement occurring. However, this borrowing is limited to ideas and concepts. Any direct copying of the work itself is illegal. Although the line is sometimes hard to draw, the following example might be helpful.

You design a wonderful new combination spread sheet, word processor, and data base program, which you call "Wordbasecalc." One of the many wonderful and marketable features of your new work is its ability to operate in less than half the time and space of other available programs, which perform only one-third as many tasks. You can accomplish this primarily because your tremendous insight allowed you to realize that the built-in operating system contained most of the functions for the spread sheet and word processor, as well as 40 percent of the vocabulary for the data base and word processor. You register your copyright to your program and begin marketing it. Although it is a big success, two other programs that claim to do everything yours does soon appear on the market.

In the first program, "Copycatcalc," your work is clearly evident. Although all of the variables and line numbers in the BASIC section have been changed, the program is otherwise nearly identical, and most of the object code in the machine language section is the same. Additionally, following the advice of your attorney, you embedded nonfunctioning code including an encrypted copyright notice in the middle of your object code. Although the code is completely useless and does absolutely nothing as far as the operation of the program is concerned, the supposedly new Copycatcalc contains this code. From this evidence, a court would probably conclude that your program was copied, and you would win an infringement suit. (To see what that can mean, turn to Chapter 15.)

In the second program, "Freeideacalc," your concept of utilizing the operating system has clearly been used, but there is no evidence that any of your code was copied. Certainly, some of the access routines into the system are nearly identical, because that is the only way in which the procedure can be accomplished, but overall the structure and program flow are different. Clearly, the new author took your ideas and created his or her own independent program from them. Consequently, there is no copyright violation here. While you might have been able to protect your idea to a limited extent by trade secret rules and nondisclosure agreements in contracts, once the concept becomes generally known, it is available for public use as long as no copyright violations occur. There is virtually no effective way to keep others from using an idea once it ceases to be secret. (For a further discussion of trade secrets, see Chapter 20.)

INDEPENDENT CREATION

The above example also demonstrates another method by which someone else can produce a similar program, or other work for that matter, and still not violate your copyright. Even a valid copyright does not prevent another from independently creating the same or an extremely similar work. This is because the very nature of copyright protection is that of preventing unauthorized copies. Unlike patents, which actually give the inventor a monopoly on the invention, copyright merely prohibits others from copying your work without your permission.

It is conceivable that two works could contain identical code and yet neither was copied from the other. Of course, the more complex a work is, the less likely it is that anyone will believe that two people independently created an identical program. (Chapter 15 considers the necessary proof of infringement in a little more detail.) However, it is well settled that copying may be inferred from the circumstances, and where the infringer has had access to the work and the alleged copy is very similar a court can be justified in finding that actual copying took place.

UNINTENTIONAL COPYING

There is no requirement that the illegal copying be intentional. For example, ex-Beatle George Harrison was found to have unintentionally infringed on the copyright of another artist by unconsciously copying the melody of "He's So Fine" in his song, "My Sweet Lord."[1] The court specifically found that Harrison did not mean to plagiarize another songwriter, but that it was evident that he had access to the other work and that with that knowledge he unconsciously violated the earlier copyright. Harrison was required to pay significant damages.

REVERSE ENGINEERING

Since copying is what is primarily prohibited, it is completely legal for someone to take a copyrighted program apart (without making unauthorized copies), study it to see how it works, and then create another program that accomplishes the same result but does it in a different manner. This process is frequently referred to as reverse engineering because you start with an end product and one means of obtaining it and then develop another method for producing the same result. More than just the use of an idea is involved, since only by studying the original is the next generation produced. However, as long as no copying of the first program has occurred, there has been no copyright violation. Indeed, in many instances the second product incorporates additional features, which, at least to some, make it worth even more than the first.

A good example of this kind of activity, and one that also involves certain patents, can be found on the hardware side of the computer industry. A number of very large companies that have invested millions and whose net worths are considerable produce IBM-plug-compatible products. This generally means that the product will work in the same situations and circumstances as the IBM product, but it is not a duplicate of such. Frequently the second company will add extra features or sell at a lower price than the first.

A similar phenomenon may be occurring in the microcomputer field today. You need only to open any micro magazine to see advertisements for a plethora of microcomputers that tout compatibility with the IBM personal computer. If these are the result of reverse engineering and do not copy valid copyrighted software, then there should be few legal problems for the manufacturers. Note, however, the legal battle between Apple Computer, Inc., and Franklin Computer Corporation, discussed elsewhere.

The same considerations apply to application software. Undoubtedly, some of the programmers who ultimately wrote the later spread sheet programs for microcomputers studied the first Visicalc program to see how it was done. After that, they may have developed their own means of obtaining a similar end. Again, as long as there was no copying, no one's copyright was infringed.

UTILITARIAN WORKS—USEFUL ARTICLES

Works that are purely utilitarian are not susceptible of copyright. Traditionally, these have been referred to as useful articles, and the Copyright Act specifically defines these as articles "having an intrinsic utilitarian function that is not merely to portray the appearance of the article or to convey information." Examples of useful articles include industrial designs, such as lighting fixtures, and business forms.

Although most experts feel that a computer program is more than just a useful article as contemplated by this section of the act, this issue, along with many others, was raised in connection with the suit by Apple Computer, Inc., against Franklin Computer Corporation. By initially denying a preliminary injunction, which would have prohibited further sale and distribution of Franklin computers, the court noted that an operating system could be considered an essential element of a machine and the object code in its binary form or ROM form "a useful version of the machine's electrical pulse." As such, the court indicated the possibility that those particular forms of those specific programs might not be expressions, which would be subject to copyright protection. (Since only a preliminary injunction was involved, the court was not required to decide the substantive issue at that time, but only refused to block sales while the case was in progress. This decision was reversed on appeal and the case was subsequently settled.)

SOLE METHOD—LACK OF ORIGINALITY

As mentioned in the example in Chapter 7, there are sometimes certain routines in a program that can only be accomplished in a particular fashion. It has been held that where there are only a very limited number of ways in which a particular idea can be expressed, there might not be an infringement, even though the second work is very similar to or an apparent copy of the first. This situation has occurred in connection with the instructions to certain games.[2]

The concept of a game, like any other business idea, is not susceptible of copyright protection. However, the written instructions and the game board design generally are. Nonetheless, it is possible to strip the instructions down to the barest essentials. In such circumstances there might only be one way or a very limited number of ways in which they can be expressed. Since some originality must be present to create a valid copyright, it can be argued that in these situations there is insufficient originality to sustain a valid copyright claim.

Also, the independent creation doctrine may come into play here, as well as the basic idea-versus-expression dichotomy. If the expression is reduced to the barest idea itself, it would be difficult to protect with a copyright. This rule, then, can be said to be a hybrid of several others. Furthermore, if there are indeed only a few ways in which a particular program can be written, it would seem almost impossible to prove copying.

USE EXCEPTION

Another related exception, and one that was involved in a minor uprising among Apple software users against certain software publishers, is the use exception. Simply stated, if a work must be copied to be used, it may not be susceptible of copyright protection at all. The concept dates back to 1879 and a Supreme Court case entitled *Baker* v. *Selden.*[3]

A particular method of bookkeeping was developed by an author who incorporated the necessary forms into his book. He sought to prevent anyone from using those forms without first paying him a royalty. In that particular case, however, the Supreme Court held that the method (idea) of doing business could not be used without copying the forms. Therefore, the forms and the business system were absolutely useless unless the forms could be copied. In such circumstances, the Court reasoned that no valid copyright could exist because such would go beyond protection of an expression and would prohibit the use of an idea.

COMPILER PROGRAMS

In late 1981, several software companies began marketing compiler programs for the Apple II. These programs converted the user's BASIC program into machine language, which would expedite program execution significantly. Although the program to be compiled would belong to the user because certain portions of the compiler program were necessarily incorporated into the finished product, many of the producers initially indicated that they would require a license and the payment of a fee to use the compiler to produce marketable programs.

The theory originally advanced by the producers of these programs was that their copyright would be infringed because a part of their program had to be copied for the system to work. Since this run-time routine was copyrighted, the compiled program would necessarily contain a copy of part of the original copyrighted work. Under the use doctrine it is unlikely that such a provision in the sales agreement would have been enforceable, and infringement also seemed unlikely. As a practical matter, it was also impossible to enforce or even deal with, and within months all of the companies involved had given up on the idea.

FAIR USE

Recognizing the fact that there are certain occasions on which someone may legitimately quote (copy) from a work that should not subject the copier to penalties, the fair use doctrine was developed. Although not likely to be a serious consideration in connection with computer programs, fair use includes such things as reviews and critiques in which it may be necessary to copy a part of the work in order to discuss it. The extent of the copying, the purpose, the nature of the work, and the effect on the market are all considerations used to evaluate whether such an action constitutes fair use.

There are also provisions for certain library copies to be made to enrich the Library of Congress, although this does not apply to programs submitted in machine-readable form. Additionally, the copy in the archives of the Copyright Office is not deemed to be an infringement.

RIGHTS OF THE OWNERS OF COPIES

Another limitation on the extent of copyright involves the rights of the owner of a copy of the work. Although there was considerable discussion about whether the mere act of entering the program into RAM constituted a copyright violation (and this was used as an argument that computer programs should not be susceptible of copyright), the 1980 amendment clearly states that such is not the case. Additionally, the rightful owner of a copy is granted the specific right to make a copy for archival purposes.

This right to make an archival copy is a clear recognition of the danger of having your only program disk bomb with no backup. It has also fueled the controversy regarding software piracy and the subindustry devoted to creating methods by which supposedly uncopyable programs are copied. Since any rightful owner is entitled to make one copy, there is no copyright violation involved in breaking a protection scheme to do so. However, making other copies and distributing copies are other matters entirely and are not sanctioned by the act.

NOTES

1. *Bright Tunes* v. *Harrisongs, Ltd.,* 420 F.Supp. 117 (S.D. N.Y. 1976).
2. *Morrisey* v. *Proctor & Gamble,* 379 F.2d 675 (1st Cir. 1967).
3. *Baker* v. *Seldon,* 101 U.S. 99 (1880).

11. Protection for Visual Displays

In addition to obtaining a copyright for the written expression of the program, the visual display may be susceptible of copyright protection. This can be one means of getting around the reverse engineering rules. That is, if you obtain a valid copyright on your visual display, even if another programmer accomplishes the same result using a completely different program, he or she will be prohibited from distributing the work because your copyrighted display was copied.

This is because the actual audiovisual representation on the screen becomes the protected work. It really doesn't matter if different code was used, since the result is a copy of a previously copyrighted work. As will be discussed at greater length later in this chapter, Atari has used this argument in connection with certain games that had displays similar to those of "PAC-MAN." Indeed, most of the suits decided regarding video games have involved a copyrighted computer video display.

REQUIREMENTS

Not all screens are copyrightable. All of the requirements for copyrightability, such as originality, expression, and fixation, must be present. For example, a Visicalc display, absent the actual numbers, is just a computerized representation of an accountant's worksheet. There is insufficient originality to qualify this kind of screen as a copyrightable audiovisual work.

Additionally, such a spread sheet display would undoubtedly be considered a utilitarian article and would probably also be classified as something that cannot be used without being copied. (This is only with reference to the spread sheet format; clearly, you do not have to copy the program code to use the program.) Consequently, it is highly unlikely that anyone will attempt to argue that a spread sheet display is a visual or graphic display that can be copyrighted independently of the program that generates the screen. However, most original screens and displays developed for computer games would probably qualify.

STILL SCREENS

The specific forms that must be completed and the types of copies that should be sent to the Copyright Office in connection with these visual works will be covered in greater detail in Chapter 17. It should be noted that there are several different situations involving computer displays that might occur, and the treatment of each differs slightly.

For example, you may have designed a cover or title page that simply loads into the machine and sits there for a few seconds while the master program is loaded. This screen may, however, contain some of your best art, which you don't want copied without your authority. Luckily, the copyright law provides a solution. This screen is as protectable as any other drawing, painting, or graphic work. You just complete a different form from the one used for computer programs, submit a copy of the art (usually a screen dump or photograph), which is the work in this case, and send in your money. Of course, an appropriate copyright notice must appear on the screen to avoid loss of protection by publication.

MOVING DISPLAYS

What if your visual art moves? In most computer games the display is constantly changing, shapes are moving, rayguns are blasting, and monsters are being destroyed. Again, there is an analogy to works that have long enjoyed copyright protection—movies. Motion pictures include both sound and visual movement, just as do many computer games. They are both registerable using the same copyright form. In fact, the deposit copy for a computer game display that changes or moves is usually a film of such.

Another possible problem involves works that contain elements of different types of works. In these cases, the works are still susceptible of copyright, at least to the extent that there is copyrightable material contained in the work. The particular application will be determined by the most significant aspect of the work. For example, in almost all cases of computer game graphics combined with text, where the most important part of the game is the graphics rather than a textual narrative, the work will be considered an audiovisual work rather than a textual one.

HUMAN VS. MACHINE

Although computer-generated graphics displays can be the subject of a valid copyright, the mere term *computer-generated* causes additional problems. As has been seen, only original works of authorship can be the subjects of copyright. A computer cannot be an author, at least not at this time. Consequently, the Copyright Office will not accept a registration for a screen display or game that is "created" by the computer as opposed to being created by a human being. Although the difference may be subtle, it is important, particularly considering the fact that you may be requested by the Copyright Office to explain your registration application.

Apparently, what is most significant is the fact that a human being created the visual images first. It doesn't matter that the computer recreates those images out of electronic impulses. It is the initial act of creation that is important. A human being must be the one who expresses the idea initially, although the same expression can be created by the machine thereafter, for the work to be copyrightable. After all, subsequent reproduction, whether of a computer program, a computer display, or a book, is almost always accomplished by a machine recreating a duplicate of the original. In this case, however, the original becomes embedded in the computer code.

The situation in which an individual creates a screen or designs a video game is treated differently from one in which the computer independently generates a display. Although the computer cannot truly act independently, since it can only respond to programming written by humans, it is possible to write a program in which the computer creates images that were not even contemplated by the author of the program. For example, using a simple random number function to create or change designs on the screen would be an example of a visual display in which the programmer did not create the design. It is possible, therefore, that copyright registration would be denied, although there have been some decisions finding that the fact that a display changed each time the game was played, depending on the player, does not defeat copyright in the display. (This problem with computer-generated designs would still have no effect on the validity of the copyright for the program. We are dealing here only with the display.)

Even these explanations are not completely satisfactory, however. Why can't an artist use a tool to help him or her create a visual work? The answer, of course, is that he or she can. Then isn't the computer just such a tool and its use just an aid to the artist? Is there really a difference between a painter using mechanical devices to achieve certain designs on a canvas and a programmer using the random number generator in the computer, or any other feature, to assist in creating a picture? These questions will have to be resolved in the near future. In the meantime, you should at least be aware of the potential problems.

ADVANTAGES OF COPYRIGHTING GRAPHICS

Copyrighting the graphics of a program, particularly a computer game, has some distinct advantages. Circumventing possible reverse engineering has already been mentioned. Since it is the resulting visual display that is actually copyrighted, the same display cannot be obtained through another means without infringing on the first copyright. Additionally, this protection can be obtained regardless of whether a copyright is obtained for the main program. In this way, an author could choose to rely on trade secret protection for the actual program and still obtain a copyright for the display. If the protection and limitations on the program were sufficient to keep it from the would-be copiers, the copyright on the visual display would prevent them from arriving at a similar result.

A valid copyright on the graphics may also help to establish use and publication of the display in the event that someone else attempted to improperly cash in on your game's popularity. In a suit for unfair competition, similarity of ideas and products plays an important part. So does the date on which you first started using your distinctive marks and products in the marketplace.

EXTENT OF VISUAL PROTECTION

Like other forms of copyright, the protection afforded visual works extends only to the expression and not the underlying ideas. Similarly, only unauthorized copying is forbidden, and all of the other exceptions to protection, such as independent creation, use, and utilitarian articles, also apply. Of course, determining exactly where the expression is and what the ideas are, as well as applying the other rules mentioned, can be very difficult. The standard to be used in determining when an infringement has occurred in these situations has been described as "whether an average lay observer would recognize the alleged copy as having been appropriated from the copyrighted work."[1] Some of the recent cases involving Atari demonstrate the difficulties involved.

When Atari sued North American Philips over alleged infringement on its "PAC-MAN" game by the other's "K. C. Munchkin," the trial court initially held that the two games were not substantially similar and that K. C. Munchkin was derived from a different source. On appeal, however, a higher court determined that "although not virtually identical to PAC-MAN, K. C. Munchkin captures the total concept and feel and is substantially similar to PAC-MAN." Although speaking in terms of concept, the court apparently felt that the expression had been copied as well. In a similar situation, however, another court disagreed.

ATARI also sued the makers of a game called "Jawbreaker."[2] There the court found that Jawbreaker did not violate the PAC-MAN copyright and stated:

> There is nothing protectable under the copyright law as to the "PAC-MAN" game itself, and the laws do not protect the strategy of a player symbol being guided through a maze appearing to gobble up dots in its path while being chased through the maze by several opponents. Further, the unprotectable idea includes the rules, strategy, and progress of play of the "PAC-MAN" game.

Obviously, these answers are not always clearcut. Even experienced courts have difficulties in sorting out the rights of the respective parties. Where such obviously divergent opinions exist, it is very difficult for the programmer and software author to know exactly what to do. However, it is very important to be as well informed as possible and to know the steps that can be taken and their likely results.

NOTES

1. *Nintendo of America* v. *Bay Coin Distributors,* Copyright Law Decisions, par. 25,409, no. CV-82-1153 (E.D. N.Y. 1982).
2. *Atari* v. *Williams,* no. CV-F-81-410 MDC (E.D. Cal. 1981).

12. Works for Hire

WHEN YOUR WORK ISN'T YOURS

Although the general rule is that the author owns all exclusive rights to a program by virtue of creating it, this is not true in all cases. The most common example is referred to as the "work for hire" exception. The Copyright Act provides that works made for hire are generally the property of the employer. The employer, not the author, has the exclusive right to register the copyright to the work.

Generally, a work is made for hire when it is prepared by an employee within the course and scope of his or her employment. If an in-house (employee) programmer is assigned the task of developing a new word processor for the Apple, the rights to that program belong to the employer, not to the programmer. The employer is considered to be paying the employees for their expertise and should enjoy the fruits of the work he or she has paid for. However, if the programmer develops the program outside the scope of his or her job, then it belongs to that employee, unless he or she has a different and specific contractual arrangement with the employer.

A programmer should carefully read all documents presented for his or her signature when he or she begins working for a new employer. In addition to the tax, insurance, and personnel forms, important agreements such as these may be part of the package. If the meaning of a document is not clear to you, ask questions. Only after completely understanding the rights that are being relinquished should such an agreement be made.

LIMITATIONS

Since the law is designed to protect the author's interests, not all programs developed become the property of the employer. The law requires that the work be within the scope of the developer's employment. At first blush it may seem that this completely eliminates the possibility of a programmer who is working for another to ever have any rights himself or herself alone. However, even in situations involving in-house programmers, a number of problems can develop. For example, many programmers may moonlight or develop software that is not part of their jobs. Sometimes the author may even use the computer of his or her employer in connection with a program he or she is developing on the side. Who owns the copyright in such instances?

There is a strong public policy favoring copyright ownership of the author. Consequently, most courts have held that a program developed outside the scope of the programmer's employment belongs to the author, not the employer. Even where some use has been made of the employer's facilities, since the employee generally has legal access to such unless a specific contractual agreement prohibiting the use of the facilities has been reached, the employer cannot claim ownership on this basis. Nor have the statutes or the courts been willing to grant the employer any rights similar to the shop rule found in patent law, which would allow the employer the use of the invention without the necessity of paying a royalty if it was developed at the employer's shop, although the inventor still would have the exclusive rights to the invention as far as the rest of the world is concerned.

CONTRACTS

Some companies require new employees to sign an employment contract stating that any programs conceived or developed while the programmer is employed become the property of the employer, even if such was done outside the office. Whether such an agreement can be enforced depends on the particular circumstances involved.

The general rule is that parties are free to put whatever provisions they want in their contracts, so long as they are not illegal or contrary to public policy. Although it can be argued that such a blanket grant of all rights to the employer runs counter to the public policy favoring these rights in the original author, as long as the agreement was bargained for and did not involve any overreaching or unconscionable conduct, it is probably permissible. Unconscionability is discussed in further detail in Chapter 24 in connection with warranty limitations. However, many of the same considerations apply here.

CONTRACTUAL WORKS FOR HIRE—NONEMPLOYEES

The parties may contractually provide in a written agreement that a certain work is made for hire. In this situation, however, the work must fall within certain categories, such as contributions, translations, compilations, instructional texts, and supplementary works. Unless the program comes within the exception, it belongs to the author. The law is quite specific and requires the following before such will be considered a work made for hire:

> A work specially ordered or commissioned for use as a contribution to a collective work, as a part of a motion picture or other audiovisual work, as a translation, as a supplementary work, as a compilation, as an instructional text, as a test, as answer material for a test, or as an atlas, if the parties expressly agree in a written instrument signed by them that the work shall be considered a work made for hire.

APPLICABILITY TO SOFTWARE

There are several sets of circumstances where these rules can come into play in connection with software development. One of the most common situations in the microcomputer software industry involves the translation of a program from one machine to another. For example, a program written for an Apple II computer will usually not run on a Radio Shack TRS-80 without substantial modification, particularly if graphics are involved.

However, a programmer who is a whiz on one machine may not know much about the other. Another programmer must be hired to do the conversion to sell the product in this other market. Therefore, this provision prevents this part of the copyright from transferring, even if the new work is so different that it might be considered another work. Although the other requirements for a transfer, such as the necessity of a writing, would apply, since this is really not so much a transfer as a derivative work, a specific provision certainly avoids unnecessary confusion.

In an earlier discussion it was noted that the right to make translations belongs to the copyright owner. That right applies here also. Another reason for this separate provision is that the situation under consideration is more than just a simple compilation and can cover a great deal of other possibilities as well. However, any contract attempting to modify or specify these rights must be in writing, as all contracts should be.

Other areas that may be involved in works for hire include instruction manuals for programs as well as subparts to larger works. Many business software packages include several programs, which might be authored by more than one programmer. Indeed, a publisher may want to include certain additional functions in a program for which the original author either can't or won't devote the necessary additional time and effort. The publisher will then contract with another programmer for the additional material. This would be considered a contribution and, if expressly stated in the contract, a work for hire.

OTHER TRANSFERS

The Copyright Act provides that the author or other owner of the copyright can transfer those rights only by a written agreement. A verbal transfer is ineffectual. This is designed to protect the original copyright owner, who will usually be the author, from any inordinate pressure from large companies and publishers. The doctrine of unconscionability, discussed in Chapter 24, might also apply if the contract provisions were particularly onerous and the bargaining power very disproportionate.

Additionally, the added need for a written contract in the long run should reduce the possibilities of misunderstanding to the benefit of all concerned. This requirement has long been followed in real estate transactions as well. With concepts as difficult to pin down as intellectual property and software, it can easily be seen why similar provisions were incorporated into our copyright law. The different methods by which a copyright may be transferred and the effect of such will be covered in more detail in the next chapter.

13. Transfers of Copyright

METHODS OF TRANSFER

Specific examples of some of the various kinds of contracts that might involve transfers or modifications of certain rights to a program are covered in later chapters. In this chapter, the legal requisites for an effective transfer will be considered. These are the general rules that must be followed whether the transfer takes the form of a sale, a lease, or a license, and regardless of whether the transfer is for all or some of the rights granted to the copyright owner. Although the parties to a contract are usually free to incorporate any terms they desire, the law has determined that the rights involved here are significant enough to derogate slightly from that general rule. Unless certain prescribed actions are taken, a contract that was so laboriously negotiated may be worthless.

NECESSITY OF A WRITING

Basically, whether the transfer is of all rights or only of certain aspects of the different prerogatives of the copyright owner, no transfer or grant can be effective unless it is in writing or occurs by operation of law. Although the act of transfer need not be in any particular form, some written document must be used. Section 202 provides:

> A transfer of copyright ownership, other than by operation of law, is not valid unless an instrument of conveyance, or a note or memorandum of transfer, is in writing and signed by the owner of the rights conveyed or such owner's duly authorized agent.

This requirement is contrary to the general rule that people may dispose of their personal property without any formality. Another exception to this rule involves real estate. Presumably, these intellectual rights merit the same special consideration as land.

By extension, since the author must sign a written document to transfer effectively any part of his or her copyright, if an agent signs for the author, the agreement between the author and the agent giving the agent the power to so transfer valuable rights should be in writing. The document should stipulate that the agent does specifically have this power of alienation.

TRANSFER BY OPERATION OF LAW

The "by operation of law" language is primarily designed to cover inheritance and provide for the rights of the heirs when the author does not leave a will. It would be an anomaly to have the death of an author destroy the value of the copyright simply because he or she had not written a will to provide the necessary writing to effectuate the transfer.

Again, the analogy to property law is useful. Although a writing may be needed to transfer ownership rights in land, such property can also be inherited. No writing by the owner transferring the ownership is required, though succession proceedings provide a means of officially recognizing the rights of the heirs and placing the transfer on the public record.

TERMINATION OF TRANSFERS

Unlike most contracts, an assignment of copyright or any part thereof is subject to termination by the original owner of the copyright. This is true even if the owner has agreed to reassign his or her rights to the same party and even though he or she may have agreed not to terminate the arrangement. There need be no defect in the original agreement. This is simply an additional statutory right given to the author alone. It is completely one-sided, since no reciprocal right exists in favor of the transferee.

The law embodies the strong public policy expressed in the Constitution that creativity should be rewarded by granting exclusive rights to the creator. The right of termination furthers this policy by giving the author additional bargaining power. If the publisher has lost interest, the author can reclaim his or her rights and find another publisher. If the work is a great success, the author may be able to gain even more favorable terms for future distributions of the work. However, there are a number of qualifications to this right of termination, and very specific rules must be followed in order to take advantage of these provisions.

Time for Termination

The first limitation on the right of termination renders it unlikely that it will be used very much in connection with microcomputer programs. This right does not come into being until 35 years after creation of the work. If the work is published, the time limit is 35 years from publication or 40 years from creation, whichever comes first. Since there are very few computer programs, or computers for that matter, that are 35 years old, there are no precedents with respect to this aspect of the copyright law as it pertains to computers. Also, with the rapid advances being made in the industry, it seems a new generation of machines emerges every five years or so, making programs that will remain commercial for years unlikely. Nonetheless, particularly in connection with specific programs written for business, or general-purpose programs written for ubiquitous computers, there are possibilities of this rule coming into play.

For example, there are probably some programs that were written for IBM mainframes back in the 1950s that, because of the amount of time and money spent, are still being used today. Also, it seems that Visicalc and similar programs will be with us for a very long time. When you remember that the translation of a program from one language to another may be covered under the original copyright, even the introduction of more advanced machines may not eliminate the need for certain programs. Consequently, the termination rights granted under the act may become very important. We'll just have to wait and see.

Procedures for Termination

Not only does the right to terminate not come into existence until after 35 years, but the author has only five years after that in which to exercise his or her right of termination. Although five years is a long time, after 35 years it is likely that an author may not be keeping a precise watch, and so the time limit seems reasonable. More importantly, there are very specific procedures that must be followed and other requirements to be met for an effective termination under this section to occur.

It is strongly recommended that a professional be consulted if this situation ever occurs. For informational purposes, however, the procedures involved include giving written notice within the five-year period after 35 years; providing in that notice the date when such termination shall become effective, which date must be not more than ten nor less than two days after the notice; and filing a notice of the termination with the Copyright Office in accordance with its regulations before the effective date of the termination. If these procedures are followed correctly, the termination will become effective, notwithstanding any agreement to the contrary. It is because of this very special and powerful right granted to the author to abrogate a valid contract that it is imperative that these forms and procedures be followed to the letter.

In the case of an author who is deceased at the time when this termination right becomes effective, the majority of the heirs to the copyright can still exercise his or her rights. In fact, the Copyright Act even specifies who shall inherit these rights, so local law should be consulted to resolve any conflicts. If all of the heirs shall inherit, or in cases where there are more than one owner of the copyright, the law provides that a majority of the copyright owners may act if unanimity cannot be obtained. The specific rules set forth in the act should be consulted for each situation.

After termination, the copyright may be treated like any other copyright. It may be sold or reassigned to anyone, including the party whose rights were just terminated by the author. This could be a good bargaining tool. However, to ensure that the author will have this right, the act makes earlier agreements to reassign ineffectual. A retransfer can be made only after termination.

CARE IS THE KEY

Care must be taken in dealing with this section to avoid loss of important rights. The importance of following these procedures exactly is underscored by the very words of Section 203:

> Unless and until termination is effected under this section, the grant, if it does not provide otherwise, continues in effect for the term of the copyright provided by this title.

Therefore, although this powerful right of the author to terminate a contract exists, only by carefully following the rules set out in the act can such a termination be effective.

14. How to Keep from Losing a Copyright

PUBLIC DOMAIN

While almost everyone has heard of the term *public domain*, most nonprofessionals are confused about its precise meaning and the legal ramifications involved. Once a work enters the public domain—whether it is a book, an article, a song, or a computer program—it is fair game. The original author no longer enjoys the exclusive rights of reproduction, adaptation, and publication that are guaranteed to a copyright holder. Once the material is in the public domain, the author loses all of the exclusive rights discussed previously. Anyone may copy, distribute, or even sell the work in question without penalty of infringement.

Similarly, once in the public domain, that particular work cannot be retrieved and again made the proper subject of a copyright claim, although adaptations, arrangements, variations, and compilations containing the work might qualify for limited copyright protection. Even though not eligible for copyright protection, either present or future, a work from the public domain may nevertheless still be marketed. What is lost is the exclusivity of rights—the power to prevent others from reproducing the work, not the ability to sell it.

COMPUTER SOFTWARE

Although the phrase *public domain* is frequently bandied about in computer circles, there is a considerable amount of confusion about how a program becomes part of the public domain and, in effect, free. For example, there is a widespread belief among computerists that programs published in a magazine and manually typed into an individual's personal computer are in the public domain and can be reproduced with impunity. This is simply and emphatically not true.

If there is a valid copyright and an appropriate copyright notice for either the program or the magazine, the work has not been dedicated to the public. Almost every publication in which a program listing might be found is copyrighted, and the program listing is part of the written material within the magazine subject to the copyright. Therefore, the copyright notice usually found at the beginning of the magazine would be sufficient to prohibit unauthorized copying of the individual program. Similarly, there are many computer bulletin boards (electronic message centers reached by way of telephone modem) that contain unauthorized listings of copyrighted programs that are not public property. Just because a person has spent some time typing in a program does not give him or her the right to distribute that program to others, even if he or she receives no monetary consideration.

Note, however, that many magazines specifically state that permission to copy and use for the personal benefit of the purchaser of the magazine is granted. Also, most of these magazines invite the readers to type in (copy) the programs and use them for their personal, noncommercial applications. In such circumstances an implied permission may be inferred with respect to personal use and copying. However, few of these publications truly dedicate their programs to the public, and copies of such should not be given to others. Indeed, many magazine publishers also publish and sell computer software. Certainly they are not giving away for free what they are also marketing.

On the other hand, there have been cases of significant programs being accidentally placed in the public domain because of a lack of understanding of the legal requirements for protection. Much early microcomputer software was freely distributed without any regard for copyright notices. While this eliminated potential sales for the authors, it also helped to establish certain de facto standards that have helped the industry in some ways. Another good example of this type of activity is found in the various user group software libraries and user-contributed software available for such personal computers as the Apple II and the TRS-80.

HOW A WORK CAN ENTER THE PUBLIC DOMAIN

As discussed previously, Section 401 of the new act requires that an appropriate copyright notice be placed on all "publicly distributed copies from which the work can be visually perceived, either directly or with the aid of a machine or device," including a computer. Although not stated specifically in the statute, the courts have held that, by implication, copyright protection is lost when such a notice is not placed on each copy of the work. Although there are some special provisions that allow correction of certain omissions on works created after January 1, 1978, the basic rule still applies generally, and particularly to earlier works. An example that also points out the danger of relying on trade secret protection is found in *Data Cash Systems, Inc.,* v. *JS&A Group, Inc.*[1]

In *Data Cash*, a company developed a computer chess game and marketed it. Since the game unit was not a general-purpose computer but rather a self-contained unit limited to playing chess, there was no easy way for the user to view the actual program, which was contained within the ROM of the unit. To view the program would require sophisticated knowledge, since one would be required virtually to disassemble the game, remove the IC chip containing the program code, and place it into a compatible system or design one. Under these circumstances the vendor had not included a copyright notice embedded in the program or on the IC chip.

Although there was considerable debate about whether the object code of a computer program, as opposed to the source code, could be the subject of copyright at all, the appellate court decided the case based on a failure to use an appropriate copyright notice. (The lower court decision that object code is not susceptible of copyright protection, though generally thought to be incorrect today, was actually cited by the trial court in *Apple Computer, Inc.,* v. *Franklin Computer Corp.*, although that decision was specifically overruled on appeal.) Copyright protection for the chess program had been lost because of a failure to include a proper copyright notice in the program, on the actual chip, or at some other appropriate place. Therefore, the work had entered the public domain, and the direct copying of the ROM chip by another manufacturer was not illegal.

PUBLISHED AND UNPUBLISHED WORKS BEFORE 1978

Before January 1, 1978, the effective date of the new act, there was a distinct difference between the rights afforded unpublished and published works. The federal law was applicable only to published works. While the work remained in the possession of the author, it was subject to the common law of each state. Since each state's law might be different and many states simply did not provide for such protection, the situation was, at best, confusing. Furthermore, although there was no time limit for protection of unpublished works, as soon as the author relinquished possession, the possibility of losing rights upon the publication of the work arose.

Although the old act required the copyright notice only on published works, the definition of *publish* was quite broad. There was never a requirement that the work be published in the sense of having a publisher or printer engaged to reproduce the work in large quantities. Indeed, a trip to the drugstore and the use of a photocopy machine coupled with distributing copies to friends and acquaintances (even for free) can be sufficient publication to render a work public domain if the copyright notice is not affixed to every copy. Obviously, this is not what the average person considers publication, and it has been the source of considerable frustration and problems.

Because of this rather harsh rule and the desire to protect the individual who, without benefit of counsel, distributed a few copies of his or her work without a copyright notice, a limited disclosure exception was developed. Under this exclusion, if the copies actually distributed were few in number, if they were circulated to individuals who might have special status (such as colleagues or an editor asked to review a manuscript), and if an attempt to limit such distribution was made, then copyright protection was not lost. This rule was also used to protect the author upon submission of the work to an actual publisher. Since it would be quite clear that there was no intent to dedicate the work to the public (the reason for contacting the publisher quite to the contrary), the courts held that the notice was not necessary.

THE NEW ACT AND PUBLIC DISTRIBUTION

Because the earlier law referred to publication, many nonprofessionals were confused about when a notice was required. The new act more accurately expresses the law, both old and new, by using the term *publicly distributed.* There is still no requirement that there be a separate publisher or that the work be in any particular form for it to be considered to have been publicly distributed. It is, therefore, advisable to place a copyright notice on all copies of the work, rather than attempt to rely on it not having been distributed.

Placing a proper notice on all copies is advisable even if the work is unpublished. Under the earlier law, since unpublished works were not covered by the federal Copyright Act, there was some risk involved in placing a notice on them. It might make it more difficult to argue a limited distribution if some copies of the work had the copyright notice indicating that the work had been published. Also, the time limits for the duration of the copyright were computed from the date of publication, so holding off on official publication increased the time the work was protected. The new act attempts to resolve some of these problems by covering unpublished as well as published works of authorship. As discussed previously, the time period is also computed differently.

NOTICE AND TRADE SECRETS

Some attorneys feel that the placement of a copyright notice on a work may weaken any arguments that the work is protected as a trade secret. Since a trade secret must not be disclosed to the public, and the copyright notice is supposed to reflect the date of public distribution, it is feared that such a notice may be inconsistent with trade secret protection. Although there have been several cases in which courts have stated that copyright and trade secret protection are not mutually exclusive, this particular issue has not been addressed by the Supreme Court.

This problem is of no concern unless there is a real attempt to use trade secrets as a primary means of protection. Although Chapter 20 considers trade secrets in more detail, such a reliance would also mean employing methods of limiting disclosure, such as licenses and nondisclosure agreements. In such cases, a copyright notice followed by the words "an unpublished work" could be used. Since the Copyright Act does not penalize you for using a date earlier than the date of publication, the additional words should do no harm to the copyright. At the same time, they allow the argument that the work has not been published to be made in connection with trade secret efforts. (See Chapter 20 for more on trade secrets.)

WHAT TO DO IF THE COPYRIGHT NOTICE IS OMITTED

Because of the difficulties inherent in the old system, in which all rights were lost upon publication without the appropriate notice, and the reasonable misunderstandings of the nonspecialist regarding publication and distribution, the new act provides for additional safeguards. Section 405 specifically addresses the situation in which the copyright notice was omitted on publicly distributed copies. Happily, there are now several means available to avoid the loss of copyright protection.

First, a version of the limited distribution rule has been kept in Section 405(a)(1). Under that provision, copyright protection is not lost if "the notice has been omitted from no more than a relatively small number of copies. . . ." Of course, this leaves open the interpretation of "a relatively small number." Just as was the case under the old law, there will be instances in which it will be difficult to agree on what a relatively small number is. It is advisable, therefore, also to pursue the second avenue available to retain copyright protection in these circumstances.

Under Section 405(a)(2), copyright protection can be obtained for a work, even though copies have been publicly distributed without a copyright notice, if registration of the work is made within five years after such publication and a reasonable effort is made to add a notice to all copies distributed in the United States after the omission of the notice is discovered. This should make life much easier in the event that a number of copies are distributed without the notice, whether inadvertently, through ignorance, or otherwise. Although still requiring some interpretation of "reasonable effort," because of the lack of other special requirements (such as the limited distribution rules), it should be much simpler to provide for protection of works created after 1978 and distributed without the appropriate copyright notice.

THIRD-PARTY AND DELIBERATE REMOVAL OF NOTICE

There are two other instances in which the publication of a work without a copyright notice will not invalidate copyright protection. If the author or other holder of a copyright in a work contracts with another to distribute the work, and that other person or company does not place the copyright notice on publicly distributed copies, copyright protection is not lost. However, this rule applies only if there is a written agreement providing that, as a condition of the copyright owner's authorization of the public distribution of copies of the work, the copies bear the prescribed copyright notice. This rule forcefully demonstrates the need for careful review of all publishing contracts. Although the publisher frequently will buy the exclusive rights to the copyright, at least for a limited time, it is possible to grant only the right to market and still reserve the copyright to the author. In such a situation care must be taken to ensure compliance with the copyright law by the publisher, since the publisher's actions could adversely affect the author's copyright. This is a perfect example of the importance of a written contract.

Another situation in which the copyright holder's rights are still protected even though the required notice has not been placed on the copies is when the notice has been deliberately removed. Obviously, the copyright owner has no control over the copies once they are distributed with the appropriate notice. If, after buying a program, a purchaser removes the copyright notice, the copyright remains valid. This is of particular importance to computer programmers. While it is rather difficult to remove the cover sheet of a book or otherwise destroy the copyright notice on a written work without obvious defacement, it is frequently a simple matter to remove the copyright notice embedded in a computer program. These notices—in a BASIC program, for instance—would simply be a REM statement, which is a program line not needed for the execution of the program. Deleting the notice, then, would not only be extremely simple but would also not affect the operation of the program.

To avoid or at least hamper such deliberate removal of the copyright notice, some programmers have resorted to a number of tricks. In addition to the normal copyright notices at the beginning of the program listing and the first screen display, the ASCII equivalent of the copyright notice is buried in the object code. Sometimes this nonfunctioning code is further encrypted to make it very difficult for a pirate to determine its function. Consequently, it usually shows up in unauthorized copies and makes the proof of infringement much easier. Copyright infringement will be discussed in the next chapter.

NOTES

1. 203 U.S.P.Q. 735(N.D. Ill. 1979), *affirmed* 628 F.2d 1038 (7th Cir. 1980).

15. Copyright Infringement

As discussed previously, one of the exclusive grants given to an author of a copyrightable work is the right to make copies. The copyright owner may license others to make such copies, as well as granting the right to do translations and derivative works, but if someone copies the work without authority he or she has infringed upon the author's copyright and is subject to civil prosecution in a suit for copyright infringement. Depending on whether the graphics display has been copyrighted, the illegal copying may be of the program itself or of the graphics. The key word is *copy*. To prove infringement, it is necessary to show copying of a substantial nature from the original work. How then does one demonstrate unauthorized copying?

PROOF OF COPYING

Since it is unlikely that a copyright infringer will take the witness stand and confess to copying another's work illegally, the law has provided other means for proving copyright infringement. Naturally, circumstantial evidence must be used and courts must be allowed to draw reasonable inferences and presumptions from certain facts. Because of this, a number of specific rules and procedures have been developed to prove unauthorized copying.

The reasons why some special procedures must be followed also fl/ the nature of copyright protection. As previously noted, the independ/ tion of the same program will not constitute a violation. Therefore, / demonstration of nearly identical program lines by itself would not n/ prove that the defendant in such an infringement suit actually c/ original author's work. The rules relating to access come into play /

Access

To prove that another has illegally copied your program, you must first show that he or she had access to it. There have been instances involving very complicated, specialized programs, where former employees of the original copyright owner began marketing a similar and competing product. Access was easy to prove because these former employees worked on the development and implementation of the original while they were employed. In situations like this, a nondisclosure and noncompetition agreement is usually required of the employees in an attempt to avoid just this sort of problem. (Chapter 23 deals with these agreements in more detail.)

Access is not too difficult to prove in connection with mass-marketed microcomputer software, since there would be plenty of opportunity to obtain the software. Of course, it would be much better if it could be proved that the infringer actually purchased or otherwise obtained one copy and then made duplicates. However, the general availability of the program may be used to demonstrate the infringer's access.

Sometimes access will be inferred because of a defendant's position in or knowledge of a particular field. For instance, former Beatle George Harrison was held to have unintentionally copied an earlier copyrighted song, "He's So Fine," in his composition, "My Sweet Lord." Although there was no direct proof that he knew the former song, his position and stature in the music industry was such that the court felt it could reasonably presume that he knew of the earlier work.[1]

In any event, some sort of access to the work must be shown. However, this requirement is enforced less stringently where the showing of similarity to the original work is very strong. The courts have used a sliding scale with respect to the proof necessary to show access. The closer the two works are in appearance, the less proof of access is required. Obviously, the degree of similarity with the original work is of paramount importance.

Substantial Similarity

Actual copying must be proved. Although much can be done to try to cover up the duplication, if unauthorized copying has occurred the infringing work will undoubtedly be similar to the original. To be successful in proving infringement, substantial similarity must be proved. Since similarity is necessarily dependent on the particular work, precise rules are difficult to delineate, and the determination of exactly how much similarity will be required must be made on a case-by-case basis. There have, however, been several cases in the video game field that have discussed the substantial similarity requirement and can be useful in establishing some guidelines.

In one case the court enunciated the rule as follows:

> [Unlawful copying has occurred when] an average lay observer would recognize the alleged copy as having been appropriated from the copyrighted work.[2]

Precautions to Be Taken

There are a number of things a programmer can do to make the task of proving unauthorized copying (piracy) easier. However, these precautions should be taken before the program is released and in addition to the proper legal means of protecting the program by copyright, trade secret, and trademark. By combining the appropriate legal means with some of the following suggestions, a fair measure of protection can be obtained.

The fact that certain bugs that were present in an earlier version of an original work showed up in an allegedly infringing copy was strong evidence that the second work was an unauthorized copy in *Williams* v. *Artic International, Inc.*[3] Additionally, in this suit over the game "Defender," it was proved that the second work also contained the high scores of certain Williams employees, including the president, which were saved in the code by the program, and a listing of the code for the two programs showed that more than 85 percent of the code was identical. As a pièce de résistance, the infringing work actually contained a Williams copyright notice, which had been buried in the object code of the original. Under these circumstances, the court had no trouble finding that the second program infringed upon the copyright of the first.

Working from this concept, it is a good idea to place nonfunctioning code in a work for later identification. Of course, this should be documented for future reference with the program work papers and should be kept in a safe place away from intruders and would-be pirates. Since the code would be useless from a programming point of view, it is highly unlikely that another programmer would have independently created the same worthless code. Placing additional copyright notices, perhaps encrypted or otherwise hidden, is also worthwhile.

Naturally, liberal use of standard copyright notices can't hurt. A pirate, who by definition does not want to take the time necessary to create the work, may not take the time to study the program thoroughly for hidden or duplicate copyright notices. This could well be the pirate's undoing. Furthermore, as long as they are consistent, multiple copyright notices will not hurt the validity of the copyright.

PENALTIES

Copyright infringement carries both criminal and civil penalties. Fines of up to $10,000 and imprisonment for up to one year are possible penalties for a criminal conviction of copyright infringement. Since it was discovered that certain Japanese computer companies were apparently willing to pay far more than these fines to obtain American computer technology, there has been a push to make these penalties more severe. In a multibillion-dollar industry where the latest computer design can literally be worth millions, a $10,000 fine does not seem to be much of a deterrent.

However, in a private action the civil penalties and remedies will be invoked. There are several different possibilities. These include seeking an injunction to prohibit the infringer from making any more copies, an action to recover lost profits, and statutory penalties.

Injunctions

One of the most powerful remedies is the injunction. The power to prevent an infringer from marketing his or her product and thereby allowing the true copyright owner the opportunity to reap the benefits from his own work may be of utmost importance. This is particularly true in the case of extremely valuable products, such as the very expensive program for mainframes where the potential market is small and only a limited number of sales can be expected. It may also be extremely important at the other end of the spectrum. Preventing others from capitalizing on a runaway best-seller microcomputer program may be more important than seeking damages later. However, this is true only if the infringer can be stopped before too much damage is done.

Frequently, a preliminary injunction will be sought. Such an order would prohibit the alleged infringer from marketing the supposedly offending product while the litigation is pending. A preliminary injunction does not decide the issue of whether a work constitutes an infringement. It is strictly a temporary measure, although it may last for the entire length of the lawsuit (sometimes years). Because a preliminary injunction is not a final judgment, there are somewhat different considerations involved from those in connection with permanent relief.

In ruling on a request for a preliminary injunction, the court will balance the likelihood of success on the merits and the harm to the plaintiff against the effect the injunction would have on the defendant. If the original copyright holder's position seems overwhelming and there are no serious counterbalancing considerations, an injunction will be issued. However, if it appears that the defendant deserves greater consideration, perhaps because of the difference in economic positions of the parties, the request may well be denied. For example, in the *Apple* v. *Franklin* litigation, a preliminary injunction was denied by the trial court. Among other considerations, the court noted the difference in size between Apple and Franklin and determined that Apple was better equipped to contend with Franklin than Franklin was to attempt to stay in business without a product.

Monetary Damages

If the unauthorized copy has already garnered most of the market, if the market has dried up, or if an injunction is not possible, then a claim for damages from lost profits would be the primary relief requested. (A claim for damages would also normally be filed with a request for injunctive relief with respect to sales already made.) Damages may consist of several different elements, although the basic claim would be for lost profits—that is, the money that would have been made but for the infringing work. Proof of these lost profits constitutes an entire area of the law, deserving its own study. However, in a very simplified form, the basic claims that would be involved can be broken down into manageable parts.

First, the profits that the infringer made on the work may be claimed on the theory that the rightful owner would have been able to make the same sales if there were no unfair competition from the infringing work. This is also consistent with the theory of unjust enrichment. The law holds that guilty parties should not be allowed to keep the fruits of their nefarious behavior. Who better to get it than the rightful owner of the work?

On the other hand, lost profits can be proved through market studies and expert testimony regarding the probable sales that would have been made but for the unauthorized work. Of course, the best proof would be actual testimony regarding specific sales that were lost, but this is seldom available. Since all of this evidence is speculative—and the more speculative the proof, the less likely recovery will be—the Copyright Act provides for statutory penalties.

Statutory Penalties

Statutory penalties can be recovered without any proof of actual loss. Under the copyright laws, an infringer can be forced to pay $100.00 in statutory damages for each act of infringement to the copyright owner, even if the owner cannot prove that he or she lost any money at all. The primary advantage of this type of penalty is that it can be used as a deterrent.

However, the cost of litigation would be far greater than $100.00. Just filing the suit would entail far more than this. Therefore, lest the grant be totally illusory, the act also provides that the successful plaintiff can recover the court costs and attorney's fees incurred in the prosecution of the case in addition to the statutory penalties. This makes the use of this provision more possible, and, in fact, some companies have singled out well-known pirates for prosecution in the hopes of discouraging others.

Prerequisites to Statutory Penalties

Earlier, the importance of prompt filing of the copyright registration was discussed. There is another reason for expeditious action. If registration is not sought within the first three months of publication, the statutory penalties explained above will not be available in an infringement suit. This would relegate recovery to the vagaries of proof involved in a lost profits claim.

Of course, if it has been determined that the slight advantage in keeping the program secret by not registering it with the Copyright Office outweighs this problem, then this will not be a concern. However, given the overall advantages of registration and the problems involved in attempting to keep mass-marketed software secret, there seems little reason to delay filing. Again, this demonstrates the necessity of being well informed about the possible means of protection and choosing one that best suits your particular needs.

NOTES

1. *Bright Tunes* v. *Harrisongs, Ltd.,* 420 F.Supp. 117 (S.D. N.Y. 1976).
2. *Nintendo of America* v. *Bay Coin Distributors,* Copyright Law Decisions, par. 25,409, no. CV–82–1153 (E.D. N.Y. 1982).
3. No. 81–1852 (3rd Cir. 1982).

16. Do-It-Yourself Copyright Registration

Copies of each of the major forms you will need to register a proper copyright claim for a computer program, graphics display, or computer graphic art are reproduced as appendices to this book. Additional copies can be obtained free of charge by writing to:

Register of Copyrights
Copyright Office
Library of Congress
Washington, D.C. 20559

In this chapter and the next, each form and how to fill it out will be explained step by step. In this way a checklist and guideline to completing the forms will be provided for future reference.

FORM TX—LITERARY WORKS

Form TX, for literary works, is the form to use when registering a program itself—that is, when the work to be protected is the actual program, as opposed to a graphic display, whether it is written in BASIC, Assembly, FORTRAN, or any other language or in any other form. The full title of this form is "Application for Registration for a Nondramatic Literary Work." Despite the misleading title, it is the correct form to use.

The forms you will obtain from the Copyright Office, including Form TX, contain instructions regarding completion. The following discussions will expand upon those instructions and answer some of the common questions that arise in connection with completing these registration applications. A copy of the section under consideration will accompany each discussion so that ready reference can be made to the actual form. Complete copies of the forms are in the appendices. (Form TX is in Appendix A.) For clarity, an example of an actual copyrighted computer program will be used. The program is called "The Quest for the Holy Grail" and is written in Applesoft BASIC for the Apple II plus computer.

Section 1—Title

DO NOT WRITE ABOVE THIS LINE. IF YOU NEED MORE SPACE, USE CONTINUATION SHEET (FORM TX/CON)

	TITLE OF THIS WORK:	PREVIOUS OR ALTERNATIVE TITLES:
① Title	The Quest for the Holy Grail	
	If a periodical or serial give: Vol .... No .... Issue Date	

PUBLICATION AS A CONTRIBUTION: (If this work was published as a contribution to a periodical, serial, or collection, give information about the collective work in which the contribution appeared.)

Title of Collective Work: .... · Vol ..... No .... Date .... Pages ....

The title of the work should be written in section 1. Notice that if the work is a contribution to a periodical, serial, or collection, there is a separate space that must also be completed. This is necessary because there can be a separate copyright for the periodical, distinct from the copyright of the individual work. Supplying this information allows a cross-referencing of the two. The box for previous or alternative titles serves a similar referencing function.

In the case of software, the spaces seeking information regarding publication as a contribution will probably be left blank. However, if the program is published in a magazine or is sold on disk or some other media as part of an anthology of programs, these spaces should be completed with the appropriate names of the other works.

Section 2—Author(s)

There are spaces on the main form for the names and addresses of three authors. A second sheet is included for additional authors should such be necessary. In this example, two authors collaborated on the program. Therefore, each is listed as a co-author of the entire work.

Note that the form asks if the work was made for hire. As noted previously, the copyright to works made for hire generally belongs to the employer rather

② Author(s)		**IMPORTANT:** Under the law, the "author" of a "work made for hire" is generally the employer, not the employee (see instructions). If any part of this work was "made for hire" check "Yes" in the space provided, give the employer (or other person for whom the work was prepared) as "Author" of that part, and leave the space for dates blank.	
	1	**NAME OF AUTHOR:** Thorne D. Harris III Was this author's contribution to the work a "work made for hire"? Yes...... No...X	**DATES OF BIRTH AND DEATH:** Born 1950 Died......... (Year) (Year)
		AUTHOR'S NATIONALITY OR DOMICILE: Citizen of ....U.S.A......} or { Domiciled in ....U.S.A.......... (Name of Country) (Name of Country)	**WAS THIS AUTHOR'S CONTRIBUTION TO THE WORK:** Anonymous? Yes...... No X Pseudonymous? Yes...... No X
		AUTHOR OF: (Briefly describe nature of this author's contribution) Co-author of computer program	If the answer to either of these questions is "Yes," see detailed instructions attached.
	2	**NAME OF AUTHOR:** Mark Ben Hattier Was this author's contribution to the work a "work made for hire"? Yes...... No X	**DATES OF BIRTH AND DEATH:** Born 1965 Died......... (Year) (Year)
		AUTHOR'S NATIONALITY OR DOMICILE: Citizen of ...U.S.A............} or { Domiciled in ..U.S.A.......... (Name of Country) (Name of Country)	**WAS THIS AUTHOR'S CONTRIBUTION TO THE WORK:** Anonymous? Yes...... No X Pseudonymous? Yes...... No X
		AUTHOR OF: (Briefly describe nature of this author's contribution) Co-author of computer program	If the answer to either of these questions is "Yes," see detailed instructions attached.
	3	**NAME OF AUTHOR:** Was this author's contribution to the work a "work made for hire"? Yes...... No......	**DATES OF BIRTH AND DEATH:** Born............ Died......... (Year) (Year)
		AUTHOR'S NATIONALITY OR DOMICILE: Citizen of ....} or { Domiciled in .... (Name of Country) (Name of Country)	**WAS THIS AUTHOR'S CONTRIBUTION TO THE WORK:** Anonymous? Yes...... No ...... Pseudonymous? Yes...... No ......
		AUTHOR OF: (Briefly describe nature of this author's contribution)	If the answer to either of these questions is "Yes," see detailed instructions attached.

than the "true" author. In such a case the author for purposes of section 2 is the employer. There are also different rules regarding the duration of the copyright and termination. Likewise, inheritance and transfers are affected. See Chapter 12 for a more detailed explanation of works for hire.

There are also special rules that apply to anonymous and pseudonymous works, and the Copyright Office wants to know here if they apply. This might become a consideration when the programmer does business as, for example, HHH Enterprises, but has not incorporated his or her company yet still wants the copyright in the name of the company. Although he or she would be the author and would ordinarily own the copyright, the programmer could, by using the company name, let the company claim the copyright. Of course, it is easier simply to transfer the copyright by contract to the company. The law also considers as anonymous any author who is not given credit on copies of the work.

The author's date of death is required in order to compute the duration of copyright protection, and, of course, by giving the date of birth certain later assumptions may be made about the author, if necessary. Anonymous works and works made for hire use the 75-year duration rule rather than 50 years from the author's death. Because of international conventions and certain limitations regarding foreign activities, the copyright law requires the author's nationality or domicile, even if the work is pseudonymous or anonymous. For anyone living within the United States, the notation "U.S.A." is sufficient. Even if the author is not a national, if he or she is domiciled here (has a permanent residence), then "U.S.A." is appropriate.

The third line of each author's part in section 2 asks for a brief description of the author's contribution to the work. This might be something like "author of entire work," "author of music," "co-author of entire work," or "author of lines 2000 through 5000." No magic language is required—just a brief description of the author's contribution.

The Copyright Office's recent education regarding computer programs has been a source of consternation. At the time "The Quest for the Holy Grail" was registered, the Copyright Office was routinely accepting programs for registration. Although the law was the same regarding what could and could not be registered, the copyright examiners had little expertise with software. Recently, the sophistication of the Copyright Office in connection with computer software has greatly increased. Consequently, a claim of authorship of the entire work may well result in a letter requesting additional information regarding the claim and whether routines that were either previously copyrighted or in the public domain were also used. Only original material is a proper subject of copyright and registration. Therefore, these requests represent more than mere curiosity. How they are answered may affect your copyright claim.

An example of a form letter that the Copyright Office has issued, which also contains some other optional questions, is set out below:

INITIAL LETTER OF INQUIRY CONCERNING BASIS OR SCOPE OF THE CLAIM

The Copyright Office is in the process of reviewing its practices with respect to examining and registering copyright claims in computer programs. Because of the technical nature of programs themselves and the language used to describe the various aspects of creating a program, we find it necessary to seek your assistance in helping us gain a better understanding of the programs deposited for registration and the nature of the authorship represented therein.

Please be assured that the effective date of registration, which is established upon receipt of an acceptable application, deposit, and fee, will not be affected by this delay.

In the case at hand, it would be very helpful to us in examining your claim to have some additional information about the material covered by your claim.

*Option 1: First, to help better understand your comments, please describe very briefly what this program is about or what it does.

Option 2: We have questions as to the scope or extent of your claim in this program. For example, your application names the author(s) of the "entire text," and nowhere limits the claim to less than the entire work. This suggests that the program is entirely new and original and contains no substantial amount of material that has been previously registered or published or that has become standard usage for certain purposes. Although some programmers create from scratch all parts of their programs, we understand that many draw from libraries of previously developed programs or routines in creating a new program. To what extent, if any, does the work at hand contain preexisting material? Your comments will enable us better to determine whether your claim is accurately asserted or whether it needs to be limited in some way to cover less than the entire program.

COMPUTER PROGRAM GL-1

*Examiner selects option(s).

Option 3: Could you expand upon the meaning of the statement at space __ in your application (in lay terms if possible)?

Option 4: 1) Your application indicates, by stating that this is _____. Modification _____ 2) The copies you sent us suggest that this is not the first version of the present program. This raises a question as to the extent of your claim in this particular version/edition.

To be copyrightable, a work must contain an appreciable amount of creative original authorship. Where a work contains previously registered, previously published, or public domain material, the copyright in the revised version/edition covers only the additions, changes, or other new material appearing for the first time. In such cases, the new material itself must be original and contain copyrightable authorship in order to warrant registration for the revised version.

Your application names the author(s) of the "entire text" and nowhere limits the claim to less than the entire work. This suggests that the program is entirely new and original and contains no substantial amount of preexisting material, that is, material that has been previously registered or published or that has become standard usage for certain routines or purposes. However, the (1) title (2) information on the copies of this work suggests that this is a new version of a prior program. To what extent, if any, does the work at hand contain preexisting material? If this is a new version of a previously published and/or registered program, what is the extent of the new material? Your comments will be helpful in clarifying the extent of your present claim.

Option 5: Space 6 of your application indicates that the new material on which you are now claiming copyright consists of _____. Due to the technical description of the new material, we are unable to determine whether there is sufficient new and original authorship to justify a new registration.

To be copyrightable, a work must contain an appreciable amount of creative original authorship. Where a work contains previously registered, previously published, or public domain material, the copyright in the new work is based on and extends only to the new authorship appearing for the first time.

In a literary work, such as a computer program, this authorship might take the form of textual expression (letters, numbers, and symbols), compilation (the selection and arrangement of elements), revisions, and the like. The ideas, formulas, algorithms, or processes embodied in a work are not protected by copyright.

In light of the above, could you expand upon the meaning of your statement _____ or describe in less technical terms the new, original authorship in this work?

Your written comments will be most appreciated and will enable us to proceed with further examination of your claim. We would also appreciate your providing us with a phone number where we can reach you during business hours.

In your reply, please return the enclosed carbon referring to our control number.

The amount of detail you give in response to such questions is in large measure dependent on the program and the problems. Concealing information from the Copyright Office, such as failing to advise the office regarding earlier known works incorporated into the work sought to be registered, may result in a taint on the copyright sought to be protected. Full disclosure is required under the law.

In an effort to forestall such questions, it is a good idea to accompany your application for registration with a brief letter describing the program and what it does, and certifying that the claim is for original material. Note that it is possible to seek copyright registration for just a portion of the work. Also, even if the copyright examiner does not understand the work or cannot tell if it meets the act's requirement (for example, if only the object code is registered), the work will usually still be registered under the rule of doubt. This does not affect the validity of the registration but does indicate that no determination has been made about whether the work, based on its appearance, is copyrightable.

Section 3—Creation and Publication Dates

③ Creation and Publication	YEAR IN WHICH CREATION OF THIS WORK WAS COMPLETED:	DATE AND NATION OF FIRST PUBLICATION:
	Year 1981 (This information must be given in all cases.)	Date December 1, 1981 (Month) (Day) (Year) Nation U.S.A. (Name of Country) (Complete this block ONLY if this work has been published.)

This section is straightforward. Although the work may not yet have a publication date, a date of creation must always be given. Even if you have made a number of revisions while finishing the work and have changed the version number, you should still use the date you finished. If your first registration is version 3.2, do not fear. There is no real problem with this, although a brief explanation of the fact that you changed the version number during development but never produced a completed work before may avoid a letter from the copyright examiner requesting additional information. It is not necessary to file a new application every time a line of code is changed in the original program. The original copyright will still protect the work. However, major overhauls and revisions should be registered separately, either as derivative works, new versions, or completely new works, depending on the extent of the changes.

One of the major changes in the law currently being sought involves revisions. Unlike almost every other copyrightable work, computer programs tend to be modified and changed continually. Special rules specifying when additional registration is required or doing away with such additional registration may well be enacted. Until then, the rules referred to above will apply.

Section 4—Copyright Claimant

The copyright claimant will usually be the author, unless the work was one made for hire or the author has transferred his or her rights in the work to

another by written agreement. If the latter is the case, such as where an author sells his or her rights to a publisher in exchange for royalty payments on the sale of copies of the work, the statement of how the rights were transferred may be as simple as "By contract." If the author died before registration, this section might contain the words "By inheritance."

Section 5—Previous Registration

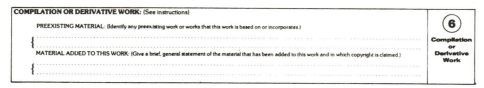

This is the section that asks if the work is 100 percent new or if at least part of it has been registered before. When building on earlier works (such as incorporating several programs into a commercial package), registering a work after publication that was previously registered in unpublished form, or registering a new version of a previously registered work, careful attention should be paid to this and the next section. Since the registration number and year of registration of the earlier work are required, it is a good idea to keep your copyright records in a secure location. Also, a notebook or other running account of changes made to registered programs, together with appropriate dates, can assist you in determining when a work becomes a new work, as well as possibly in any future infringement action.

Section 6—Compilations and Derivative Works

COMPILATION OR DERIVATIVE WORK: (See instructions)

PREEXISTING MATERIAL: (Identify any preexisting work or works that this work is based on or incorporates.)

MATERIAL ADDED TO THIS WORK: (Give a brief, general statement of the material that has been added to this work and in which copyright is claimed.)

6
Compilation
or
Derivative
Work

As mentioned above, section 6 is filled out in conjunction with section 5 for derivative works and works previously registered in unpublished form. It is also used in connection with compilations of different works as well as translations and other derivative actions. For example, a collection of utility programs previously registered by different authors might also be the subject of a separate copyright registration as a compilation. Indeed, the derivative work might well prove to be far more valuable than any of the originals simply because it brings all of the earlier works together into a more usable and marketable package. Additionally, the compilation may also contain original material that is copyrightable, such as interfacing routines and menu screens. Note that this section should also be completed if the work incorporates public domain material, which is not susceptible of copyright protection.

Section 7—Manufacturers

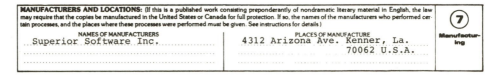

The law requires that certain copyrightable material be manufactured in the United States or Canada in order to obtain full protection, or that certain import duties may be required. This will generally not be a problem with computer software. A much more fundamental question is "Who is the manufacturer?" In most cases this will be the publisher. Manufacturing a program usually means copying that program (manufacturing the manual is the same as publishing any other book and is handled accordingly), which is usually accomplished by the publisher. If the programmer is doing this himself or herself, then he or she should be listed as the manufacturer.

Sections 8, 9, 10, and 11—Miscellaneous

Section 8 is a simple provision for allowing copies to be made for the blind and is straightforward.

The deposit account referred to in section 9 relates to certain accounts that are kept by attorneys and others who do a great deal of work with the Copyright Office. Generally, this provision will be left blank, and a check will be enclosed with the registration application.

CERTIFICATION: ⌗ I, the undersigned, hereby certify that I am the: (Check one)

☒ author ☐ other copyright claimant ☐ owner of exclusive right(s) ☒ authorized agent of: Mark Ben Hattier
(Name of author or other copyright claimant, or owner of exclusive right(s))

of the work identified in this application and that the statements made by me in this application are correct to the best of my knowledge.

Handwritten signature: (X) ....

Typed or printed name. Thorne D. Harris III .... Date Dec. 21, 1981

10 Certification (Application must be signed)

MAIL CERTIFICATE TO

Thorne D. Harris III/Superior Software Inc.
(Name)
4312 Arizona Ave.
(Number, Street and Apartment Number)
Kenner, Louisiana 70062
(City)   (State)   (ZIP code)

(Certificate will be mailed in window envelope)

11 Address For Return of Certificate

Section 10 requires a signature. While the copyright claimant should ordinarily sign, his or her attorney or other agent may do so. Note the requirement of a printed or typed name for those with illegible signatures.

Although confusing to some, the double request for a name and address in sections 9 and 11 allows for the certificate to be sent to the claimant, while correspondence regarding any difficulties may be sent to the attorney handling the application. If the application is filed by an attorney, it is important that he or she receive all pertinent correspondence so that the attorney will be aware of any complications. Any competent attorney will then relay all pertinent information to the client.

False Statements

Although it should not be necessary, a warning appears at the bottom of the form. It reminds applicants that a false statement may result in a fine of up to $2500. Moreover, inaccurate information on the application may jeopardize the copyright protection that registration is designed to assist. Care should be taken in completing the application.

MAILING IT OFF

Now that the registration application is complete, all that remains to be done is to mail it to Washington. However, along with the completed form, the following must also be sent:

1. Two copies of the work if published, one if unpublished

2. Any explanatory material necessary

3. A check for $10.00 payable to the Register of Copyrights

Be sure to insure your registration with the Post Office when you mail it, and keep the receipt until your registration is returned to you in the mail. This may take anywhere from a few weeks to several months.

DEPOSIT COPIES OF THE WORK

The copies of the program that are sent with the registration deserve a few additional comments. The Copyright Office used to accept disks and tape versions of computer programs as deposit copies. However, this presented problems of storage and review. Without the particular machine necessary to use the program it would be impossible to ascertain if the deposit copy of the work even looked like it was in proper form or was otherwise appropriate. Consequently, the Copyright Office now requires a listing or printout of the program for which registration is sought.

Although for virtually every other type of work a complete copy is required, the Copyright Office regulations allow the filing of the first and last 25 pages of computer programs in lieu of a deposit of the entire creation. For many microcomputer programs, 50 pages will more than cover the entire length of the program, so the relaxation of the deposit requirement does little good. Additionally, unless there are strong reasons for not supplying the entire work, it will be much easier at a later date to prove that unauthorized copying took place if the complete work was registered.

One possible reason for not supplying the entire work is to try to protect trade secrets. Trade secrets and the advantages and disadvantages of this type of protection are discussed separately in Chapter 20, but it is enough to remember here that any secret is only good as long as it is a secret. Therefore, if the program contains a unique algorithm that the author does not wish others to discover, placing it in the middle of a very long program and then only registering the first and last 25 pages affords some added protection.

Another important point is to include the copyright notice in the deposited materials. The act merely requires that notice be placed in a conspicuous location. This is usually at the very beginning or end of a program. Therefore, the first and last 25 pages usually contain at least one such notice. If the deposit does not contain a notice, the Copyright Office may well refuse to issue the certificate of registration. If the material being registered is the object code and the notice is such that it will be displayed when the program is run, this fact should be disclosed in a cover letter. Additionally, the printed listing of the hex code listing or source code should contain an appropriate copyright notice.

17. Completing Other Registration Forms

FORM VA—VISUAL ARTS

Another form for registration with which you should become familiar is Form VA. Form VA is used to register a copyright in a work in the visual arts. In the case of computer software, this would include graphics screens and pictures that are static. For example, many computer games begin with an elaborate picture of some aspect of the game: castles, dragons, landscapes, and so on. Such pictures may be copyrighted separately and in addition to the computer program itself. This is particularly important if the picture will be used in conjunction with a manual or advertising. In such circumstances, registration is made on Form VA.

If the screen also contains text, such as titles, instructions, or the ubiquitous "PRESS ANY KEY TO CONTINUE," Form VA is still the proper form to use as long as the predominant characteristic of the work is graphic. When the art is purely secondary to the text, use Form TX, as discussed in Chapter 16. In any event, if the wrong form is chosen, it is likely the Copyright Office will reject the application and request a resubmission utilizing the proper form.

This form is almost identical to Form TX. Indeed, the only differences occur on the second page. There you will notice that the request for the manufacturer in what was section 7 of form TX is gone. This is probably because Form VA was historically used to register fine art works, such as paintings, and those are seldom subject to mass manufacture. For similar reasons, the section referring to copies for the blind has been deleted. Therefore, sections 9, 10, and 11 of Form TX become sections 7, 8, and 9 of Form VA. A copy of this form is included in Appendix B.

FORM PA—PERFORMING ARTS

Form PA is used to register works in the performing arts. This form is appropriate when animation is sought to be protected. The form, except for the name, is identical to Form VA. Also, as with Form VA, this protection is different from the protection afforded by registering the program. Assuming that a copyrightable work is involved, what is protected is the actual combination of shapes, designs, and movements. This is the same type of protection and registration used in the motion picture industry.

In the case of arcade-type computer games, where the entire game consists of graphics animation, some people copyright only the graphics as a work in the performing arts. The actual code for the program is then kept as secret as possible, and every attempt is made to treat it as a trade secret. See Chapter 20 for a more complete discussion of the pros and cons of relying on trade secret law for protection of computer software.

If Form PA is used and the actual program code is not submitted, the deposit copy can be a video tape or film of the graphics display. Be sure to include all of the different aspects of the work. If certain movements and shapes repeat in identical sequences, it is not necessary to continue to repeat them in the copy. However, all of the different movements, pictures, and so on, should be included so that all original work of authorship is protected.

It may be impossible to record every single possible combination of shapes and motion, since these may change with the play of the game and the interaction of the player with the program. Indeed, it has been argued that such displays could not be the subject of a valid copyright because the work is not created until the play of the game. The player is actually "creating," as a co-author, part of the work simply by playing. It could not be copyrighted before that time, and any attempt at prohibiting others from using the display is inappropriate. However, the majority opinion today rejects this position in favor of granting full copyright protection for these works.

Copyright of the audiovisual part of a computer game is a powerful protective device. It protects the ultimate display, rather than the specific code, so others cannot circumvent copyright by reverse engineering. There have been a number of cases upholding this procedure in the video arcade area, and the same considerations should apply to personal computer programs. A copy of Form PA is found in Appendix C.

FORM CA—SUPPLEMENTAL REGISTRATION

In addition to the primary registration forms noted above, the Copyright Office provides forms for supplemental registrations. Form CA should be used to correct mistakes made in earlier filings or to supplement information supplied in those filings. For example, if the author's name was misspelled, a co-author was omitted, or the description of the work was incorrect, Form CA should be used to make the correction.

A supplemental registration should not be confused with new registrations that are made after the initial filing. Examples of such new registrations, which would be accomplished on the primary forms (TX, VA, or PA), include registration after publication of a work previously registered in unpublished form or registration by a new copyright claimant after transfer of the copyright. Also, if there has been any significant change in the program or display, then a new primary registration should be made. A copy of Form CA is in Appendix D.

FORM RE—RENEWAL REGISTRATION

As explained in Chapter 8, a renewal registration must be filed in order to extend copyright protection beyond the original term for works registered before January 1, 1978. The form to be used is Form RE, a copy of which is in Appendix E. Of course, considering the relatively short usable life of a computer program and the youthfulness of the industry, it is unlikely that there will be many occasions calling for the use of Form RE in connection with computer software.

DEPOSIT COPIES

Because of the nature of copyright protection, the law requires that copies of the work be submitted with the registration form. These copies are subject to public inspection, though not copying, so that it may be determined if a new work infringes on a previously copyrighted one.

Generally, two copies of the best edition of the work are required for published works, while one deposit copy must be submitted for unpublished works. Special rules with respect to computer programs allow the filing of the first 25 pages and the last 25 pages in lieu of a complete copy. For visual or audiovisual works, a film or videotape of the animation or a picture of the graphics display will suffice. In all cases, however, the submitted copy must show the copyright notice.

THE BEST EXPRESSION AND THE RULE OF DOUBT

The Copyright Office formerly accepted disks, tapes, and other machine-readable media as deposit copies in connection with computer programs. However, this practice has been discontinued, and a printout of the program is now required as the deposit for all registrations of computer programs, or at least the first and last 25 pages of such. Additionally, it is the Copyright Office's position that the source code (as opposed to object code) represents the best expression of the copyrightable matter, and such is requested for the deposit. Certainly, the source code is far more comprehensible to humans than is the object code and therefore represents the most communicative form of the work. However, if you do not want to submit the source code for secrecy or other reasons, the object code will be accepted under the rule of doubt.

The rule of doubt represents a recognition by the Copyright Office that it cannot tell if the work even has the appearance of a copyrightable work or whether the subject matter is susceptible of copyright protection when it is in object code form. However, it does not invalidate the copyright, and the work is accepted on the basis of the author's assertion that it contains copyrightable subject matter. If the object code contains an embedded copyright notice, such should be called to the attention of the Copyright Office in a transmittal letter with the submission. Also, the first page of the object code listing or, for that matter, the source code or BASIC listing should contain a copyright notice. If the notice is to be placed on a ROM chip, disk, or other media, a copy, photograph, or drawing of such placement should also be submitted.

Part Three

OTHER FORMS OF PROTECTION

18. Trademarks and Trade Names

ADDITIONAL PROTECTION

In addition to the protection afforded by copyright, it is sometimes advisable to protect the names under which a product is marketed. Have you ever wondered what the TM or the ® behind the name of your favorite soft drink (or software) really meant? Do you know why there has been so much controversy over the Pineapple, Pear, and HMS–80 computers? Or why some companies have been forced to change either their own names or the names of their products because of conflicts with the names of other companies or products? The answers to these questions and the reasons behind the changes are generally found in the law of trademarks, trade names, and unfair competition.

WHAT IS A TRADEMARK?

A trademark can be any sign, symbol, word, or other mark or device, which is attached to goods offered for sale in the marketplace in order to identify that merchandise with a particular manufacturer or seller. In many respects it is a substitute for the autograph of the author or seller, certifying genuineness or authenticity of the product. When a mark is associated with a particular merchant, it is his or her trademark. (For those primarily concerned with providing the public with a service, there is also a service mark. The considerations and registration are similar.)

A trademark does not guarantee quality or value, however. Its function is solely to indicate ownership or origin and to afford the owner of the trademark protection against the sale by others of similar or the same product as the owner's with the same or a confusingly similar designation. As such, it is designed to protect the good will of the owner and prevent the passing off of ersatz products.

RIGHTS OF THE TRADEMARK OWNER

Generally, the trademark owner possesses the exclusive right to use his or her trademark and can prohibit others from using it or a deceptively similar mark in connection with the sale of the same type of goods in the area in which his or her trademark is valid. It differs from copyright in a number of respects. The most fundamental difference involves the basic concept of use. A trademark is only valid if it is being used. A person may not coin a trademark, register it, and then prohibit others from using it. Unlike copyright protection, which provides that once the work is created others are prohibited from copying it, a trademark must be in actual use before the owner can prohibit others from using it.

Trademarks only pertain to particular products. Most readers of this book will be familiar with Apple Computer's trademarks on Apple II, Applesoft, and the multicolored apple symbol. However, the existence of such trademarks generally cannot be used to prohibit the use of similar terms in connection with totally unrelated subjects. Apple Computer might be hard pressed to stop a maker of products derived from the fruit of the apple tree from using Apple II as the name for its second apple pie product. On the other hand, a mark that may not be identical but might cause confusion in the public mind as to who made the product would be prohibited, even if was not a direct copy of one of the Apple trademarks. The test is usually whether an ordinary person would be deceived about the origin of the product.

USE, PRODUCT, AND TERRITORY

Trademarks exist by virtue of use. And use means the actual sale of the product in the marketplace under the trademark, preferably with the mark affixed thereon. Without such sales, there can be no protection, either state common law or federal. In the case of federal protection, such sales must be in interstate commerce; that is, the sale must be across state lines.

Trademarks are also limited by their use regarding both product and territory. Trademarks are not valid outside the territory in which the goods bearing the mark are marketed. Consequently, it is possible that a particular company in one state has marketed its products with a certain trademark, while at the same time a different company in another state has chosen to market its goods under the same mark. If the goods are completely unrelated, there may be no problem. However, if the products are similar, an obvious conflict arises.

In such instances, the trademark usually belongs to the company that first used it in that area, even if the other company was the first to use the trademark overall. Therefore, the company that used the mark first, but second in the particular locale, may not be able to use it because of the other company's valid first use of the mark. Today, in the microcomputer software field, with nation-wide sales the norm rather than the exception, this is probably less of a problem than it once was. It could still present problems to the fledgling local business. Indeed, as software companies grow from local to national concerns, they frequently discover another company in a different state with the same or a very similar trademark or name. Some advance planning can minimize these problems.

WHO OWNS THE TRADEMARK?

Another problem stemming from the use requirement involves the concept of who owns the trademark. Generally, the user is the owner. In the case of computer software, the user is ordinarily the publisher of the program rather than the author. Although there may be an argument that the author, who has licensed the publication and sale of the work and who retains a royalty on such sales, still owns the trademark, the area is still somewhat nebulous. Consequently, this issue should be specifically addressed in any contract between author and publisher if the author desires to keep this right. Otherwise, the trademark will probably belong to the publisher.

DISTINCTIVENESS, NOT NOVELTY OR INVENTION

Unlike the prerequisites for patents, which are discussed in Chapter 19, it is not necessary to discover or invent a trademark, nor is there a requirement of novelty or that the product go beyond the prior art, as there is in patent law. What is required is that the mark be distinctive so that it may be used to distinguish these particular goods from other goods of the same type in the marketplace. Therefore, words that are merely descriptive of quality, location, style, or class of goods may not be the subject of a valid trademark unless, through longstanding use, they have acquired a second meaning.

This requirement is usually expressed as the need for the trademark to be "fanciful, arbitrary, unique, distinctive, and nondescriptive." Examples of names that were not considered unique enough include "China Clipper" used for a restaurant and "Confidential," "Consumers," and "Graphic" used in connection with a camera. On the other hand, the courts have found the requisite distinctiveness in "Coca Cola," "Clorox," and "Q-Tips."

In connection with software, it is doubtful that a word processing program by Superior Software would enjoy a valid trademark if the mark was to be

"Superior Software's Word Processor." Obviously, such a name is purely descriptive. On the other hand, "Super-Softwrite" might fare better. Generally, the less descriptive the trademark, the better it is. Words that are newly coined and do not relate to anything else are the strongest. Of course, as a practical matter, an author or publisher may want to forego the possibility of trademark protection because a descriptive title may be a better business move. It takes little advertising to convey the purpose of "Superior Software's Word Processor," while the purpose of "Super-Softwrite" may not be as obvious.

Even if the mark does not originally meet the "fanciful" requirement, it is still possible that through use the public will come to identify a certain product with a particular mark. The mark is then said to have taken on a second meaning. It is more than merely descriptive, and people would generally recognize the mark as pertaining to a particular product and company. In these cases, the proof generally will consist of much expert testimony based on surveys and market research. Product recognition can become an extremely important consideration in such instances. Naturally, each case will turn on its own peculiar facts.

PUT IT ON THE LABEL

Trademarks and trade names exist by virtue of use. Therefore, it is essential that they be used, and the law says that you use your trademark by affixing it to the product being sold. Note that the product must be sold, and to obtain federal protection it must be sold in interstate commerce with the name affixed on it. However, since some products are a little hard to write or draw on, a trademark located on the package or wrapper will suffice.

Since it may be impractical to affix your trademark on a floppy disk, it is comforting to know that your mark on the disk jacket or on the packaging will protect the trademark. Remember, the only way to acquire a valid trademark is by use. Failure to use a valid trademark once acquired can result in a finding that the mark has been abandoned.

LOSING A TRADEMARK

Since the trademark rights exist only by virtue of use, their existence is coextensive with that use. For example, your rights extend only to the types of products on which you place the mark and the locations in which you use it. If you discontinue the use of your trademark, it reenters the public domain. At that point, anyone may reappropriate the name and begin to use it, but, in contrast to a copyrighted work, such use may then form the basis for a trademark of the new user. What was once Jones's trademark can become Smith's mark and be legitimately registered as such.

Besides outright abandonment, it is also possible that a trademark may become generic and no longer protectable. This happens when the trademark becomes the name of a particular type of product. Aspirin, wax paper, and tin foil are good examples of words that were once trademarks but through general use by the public came to mean a class of products rather than an individual manufacturer's goods. This is one of the reasons why Xerox Corporation has spent a great deal on advertising to remind the public that making photocopies is not the same as making a "Xerox." Similarly, the Coca Cola Company has brought suit against a number of establishments that don't distinguish between another cola drink and "Coke." When asked for a "Coca Cola," if another soft drink is served without noting that it is not a "Coke," the unwary bar owner risks a lawsuit. One of the rationales behind this behavior on the part of the soft drink manufacturer is the fear that a proprietary trade name or trademark could become a generic term for *all* cola soft drinks.

COMMON LAW PROTECTION

Trademarks are protected by the common law and in some instances specific statutes of the various states. This means that, even without registration with the Patent and Trademark Office in Washington, a legitimate trademark is still protected. Use, rather than statutes, brings trademark rights into existence. However, registration with the government, while not creating the rights, does grant some important advantages.

It is important to note that, unlike the rules governing copyright, you may not place the notice of registration (®) on your product until after you actually receive a registration certificate from the Trademark Office. Failure to abide by this rule can result in the denial of registration. In the meantime, the TM designation can be used to signify your claim, although it is not yet officially registered.

RIGHTS GRANTED BY REGISTRATION

Although registration does not create the substantive rights, it does afford some important procedural ones. An action to enforce a registered trademark can be brought in federal court, thus gaining the benefits of the Federal Rules of Civil Procedure and the federal court system. (These procedural advantages can be significant.) Even more important to the owner, registration acts as constructive notice that the trademark is in use and shifts the burden of proof to anyone who is trying to attack a registered claim. The first registered mark is presumed to be the one first in use.

This can be a very valuable benefit, since it is often extremely difficult to prove who used the mark first and where. By virtue of registration, you start from a position of strength. Of course, since the rights are only procedural, they do not prevent another from proving that he or she used the trademark first and you are infringing on that use, but earlier registration of your mark will make it more difficult for him or her to do so. However, there are specific limitations on the grounds for attack on a trademark registered on the principal register, and after five years those grounds are further narrowed.

Additionally, registration will prevent others from registering the same mark subsequent to your registration, and it facilitates foreign registration, which sometimes requires earlier registration in the home country. Furthermore, there are procedures set up by which new marks that might infringe are subject to interference notices, and a system of determining which mark will prevail exists. Registration also entitles the registrant to use the registered symbol ®.

TRADEMARK REGISTRATION

Trademarks may be registered with:

Patent and Trademark Office
U.S. Department of Commerce
Washington, D.C. 20559

Forms for filing your application may be obtained from that office as well. Note that there are different forms for individuals, corporations, and firms (unincorporated associations). (A copy of each form is contained in Appendices F, G, and H. A completed corporation form accompanies this discussion.)

While the forms are not especially difficult to complete, it is both more expensive and a bit more time-consuming to register a trademark than to register a copyright. Additionally, the rules are more strict, and even small mistakes can be costly. Errors are not easily corrected, and, because of the extra complexity and long delays, it is frequently advisable to consult an attorney first.

There are other peculiarities and differences from copyright registration that should be noted. First, the fee is $35.00 rather than $10.00 for each class of product on which the mark is used and for which registration is sought. The written application also requires that you identify the class of goods your product belongs in, although computer software is not yet listed as a class and a description must suffice. Another possibly confusing point is the required specimens of use or drawings.

Five specimen copies showing how the trademark is used must be submitted with the registration application. These are usually labels on which the trademark is affixed. Ordinarily, disk labels should be sufficient unless there are other designs not on the labels used in advertising or selling the program.

If the trademark is comprised solely of letters and/or numerals, a drawing may be used. This is simply the words, letters, or numbers in capital letters typed

TRADEMARK APPLICATION, PRINCIPAL REGISTER, WITH DECLARATION (Corporation)	MARK *(identify the mark)*
	CLASS NO. *(if known)*

TO THE COMMISSIONER OF PATENTS AND TRADEMARKS:

NAME OF CORPORATION [1]
Superior Software Inc.

STATE OR COUNTRY OF INCORPORATION
Louisiana

BUSINESS ADDRESS OF CORPORATION
4312 Arizona Ave. Kenner, Louisiana 70062

The above identified applicant has adopted and is using the trademark shown in the accompanying drawing[2] for the following goods: __computer software and related goods and products__

and requests that said mark be registered in the United States Patent and Trademark Office on the Principal Register established by the Act of July 5, 1946.

The trademark was first used on the goods[3] on __January 1, 1983__ ; was first used on the goods[3] in
(date)

__Interstate__ commerce[4] on __January 1, 1983__ ; and is now in use in
(type of commerce)   *(date)*
such commerce.

5

The mark is used by applying it to[6] __the goods and the packaging for the goods__

and five specimens showing the mark as actually used are presented herewith.

7

__Thorne D. Harris III__
(name of officer of corporation)
being hereby warned that willful false statements and the like so made are punishable by fine or imprisonment, or both, under Section 1001 of Title 18 of the United States Code and that such willful false statements may jeopardize the validity of the application or any registration resulting therefrom, declares that he/~~she~~ is
__President__
(official title)
of applicant corporation and is authorized to execute this instrument on behalf of said corporation; he/~~she~~ believes said corporation to be the owner of the trademark sought to be registered; to the best of his/~~her~~ knowledge and belief no other person, firm, corporation, or association has the right to use said mark in commerce, either in the identical form or in such near resemblance thereto as may be likely, when applied to the goods of such other person, to cause confusion, or to cause mistake, or to deceive; the facts set forth in this application are true; and all statements made of his/her own knowledge are true and all statements made on information and belief are believed to be true.

__Superior Software Inc.__
(name of corporation)

By _____(President)
(signature of officer of corporation, and official title of officer)

__February 1, 1983__
(date)

on letter-sized bond paper. However, if the arrangement, layout, or design is significant, then the drawing should be done in India ink on bond or bristol board. Other information that must be supplied includes the date of first use, where and how it is used, an identification of the goods in question, the name and address of the applicant, and an attestation to the truth of all of this information.

Attached to the registration are five copies of the drawing. The drawing in the example, which should be on a separate page, is:

Applicant:	SUPERIOR SOFTWARE Inc.
Address:	4312 Arizona Ave. Kenner, LA 70062
First use:	January 1, 1983
Commerce:	January 1, 1983
Goods:	Computer software and related goods and products
Drawing:	USEABLE GRAPHICS

REGISTRATION DELAYS

After complying with all of these requirements, there is typically a long wait while your application is processed. Sometimes a year can pass before notice is received. This is because of the number of registrations involved each year and the fact that a search of other trademarks is made to determine if the mark submitted has been used before. (A trademark search can also be done before filing for registration by an attorney or a company specializing in such searches.)

SUPPLEMENTAL REGISTERS

If the Trademark Office rejects the claim for some reason, all is still not lost. There are supplemental registers on which your mark may be listed. These have been established primarily for the purpose of allowing a registration in this country, so foreign registrations can be obtained. Most countries require that registration be made first in the registrant's home country. The supplemental registers were designed to protect U.S. companies from the trademark blackmail that some foreign companies have engaged in. A foreign company would register a name used here and then extract a fee to sell the name back to the original owner for use in a foreign country. The supplemental registers are designed to alleviate the problem.

They also may afford some protection in connection with proof of use, even though the mark might not qualify for the full benefits granted with registration on the principal register. Generally, however, marks that are only registered on a supplemental register are not granted the numerous advantages mentioned above. Nonetheless, some protection is better than none.

The Patent and Trademark Office publishes a free booklet entitled *General Information Concerning Trademarks,* which can serve as a source for additional information on trademarks. However, neither that publication nor this chapter is a substitute for a law degree. For specific problems, an attorney should be contacted.

TRADE NAMES

Though many of the considerations are similar, trade names are different from trademarks. A trade name acts as a designation of a particular business, place, or class of goods, which does not qualify as a trademark. Trade names are not per se registrable with the Patent and Trademark Office. However, a trade name may also be a trademark if it meets all of the other requirements. In such cases, the name or mark may be registered, and all of the advantages of trademark registration are gained.

Trade names also constitute part of the good will of a business, and the law of unfair competition prevents others from capitalizing on your good name. Again, the key is whether there is a substantial likelihood of confusion in the mind of the public and if there has been an attempt to pass off goods as another's. If such has occurred, an action is possible.

Like trademarks, a trade name is only good if it is used, and then only where it is used and in connection with the manner of use. It is certainly possible for two distinct companies in two different states to have adopted the same trade name. Just because Company A was first to use the name in its state, however, does not mean that it can prevent Company B from using the same name in another state where that company might have been first to use it. Obviously, this can lead to problems.

CORPORATE AND STATE TRADE NAMES

Incorporation obviates some of these problems on a statewide basis, since a corporate charter will not be granted to two different companies with the same name. Indeed, most states have a system whereby one can write or call the secretary of state to reserve a corporate name before actually incorporating and thereby determine if the name of choice has already been taken.

Prepared and Furnished by
JAMES H. "JIM" BROWN
Secretary of State

STATE OF LOUISIANA
SECRETARY OF STATE
BATON ROUGE, LOUISIANA

**APPLICATION TO REGISTER TRADE-MARKS
AND TRADE-NAMES OR SERVICE MARKS**

Corporations Division
P. O. Box 44125
Baton Rouge, LA 70804
Phone No. (504) 925-4701

Pursuant to Revised Statutes of 1950, Title 51, Chapter 1, Part VI, as amended, relating to the registration,
renewal, use and protection of trade-marks and trade-names or service marks.

This application may be used by an individual, firm, corporation, association, union or other organization and is to be
completed and submitted to the Secretary of State in original form only.

Application must be accompanied by check or money order in the amount of $10.00 per application made payable to the
Secretary of State. Be sure to answer all questions on the form.

Refer To The Reverse Side Of This Form For General Instructions For Filing Application And For Classification.

CHECK ONE: ☐ TRADE-MARK   ☒ TRADE-NAME   ☐ SERVICE MARK
                Identifies A Product   Idenfities A Business   Identifies A Service

CHECK ONE: ☒ ORIGINAL FILING   ☐ RENEWAL

1 Name Of Person(s) Or Corporation Applying For Registration
       SUPERIOR SOFTWARE INC.
       Full Street Address And/Or P. O. Box, City, State And Zip Code Of Applicant
       4312 ARIZONA AVENUE, KENNER, LOUISIANA   70065
       If Applicant Is A Corporation, List State Of Incorporation
       LOUISIANA

2 Name Of Trade-Mark, Trade-Name, Or Service Mark Applied For By Applicant. If A Logo Is Included, Please Describe.
       SENSUOUS SOFTWARE

3 List the Goods, Services, Or Type Of Business To Which The Name Or Mark Is Applied
       COMPUTER PROGRAMS AND RELATED WRITINGS

4 Classification Number (Separate Form for Each Class) See Reverse Side Of Form
       ENTER CLASS NUMBER HERE: 50

5 State The Manner In Which The Mark Or Name Is Used In Connection With Specific Goods, Services, Or Type Of Business
       TRADENAME FOR MARKETING CERTAIN PROGRAMS

6 Date Mark Or Name Was First Used By Applicant Or Predecessor*

       DECEMBER 15 , 19 81
       Month & Day   Year

       Date Mark Or Name Was First used In Louisiana*

       DECEMBER 15 , 19 81
       Month & Day   Year

*   The Mark Or Name Must Be In Use On The Date Of This Application. Reservations Are Available For Names Not Yet In Use.
       (See Reverse Side, General Instruction No. 6)

7 If The Logo Of Your Mark Or Name Is Part Of Your Registration , Attach Three (3) Copies Of Your Logo (Design, Artwork, Sketch, etc.) here:

AFFIDAVIT

8 STATE
       LOUISIANA
       PARISH OR COUNTY
       ORLEANS

I, the applicant am the owner of the mark or name sought to be registered and no other person, firm, association, union or
corporation has the right to such use in such class, either in the identical form hereinabove described, or in any such
resemblance thereto as may be calculated to deceive, and the facsimiles or counterparts herewith filed are true and
correct.

Sworn to and subscribed before me, this ___26th___ day

of ___January___ , 19 82

Richmond Eustis
NOTARY PUBLIC

NAME OF APPLICANT
SUPERIOR SOFTWARE INC.
AUTHORIZED PERSON
THORNE D. HARRIS III
TITLE
PRESIDENT
The above named person, by his signature, swears that he is the applicant, or an
authorized representative of the applicant, named in the foregoing application, and
that the facts alleged in said application are true.

APPLICANT OR AUTHORIZED REPRESENTATIVE

Additionally, many states allow the registration of trade names. A copy of a typical state application form to register a trade name accompanies this discussion. Note that this particular form can also be used as a state registration for a trademark. By registering in this fashion, many of the procedural benefits gained nationally through registration of a trademark can be obtained on a state-by-state basis for trade names, usually at a moderate cost.

19. Patents

WHAT IS A PATENT?

A United States Letters Patent constitutes a grant of a legal monopoly on a particular invention, machine, or process. When issued, it results in the holder having the exclusive right to make, use, and sell the substance of the invention for up to 17 years, depending on the invention. A short pamphlet entitled "What Is a Patent?" describes in layman's language some of the fundamentals of patent law. It is available for $1.00 per copy from:

American Bar Association
Section of Patent, Trademark, and Copyright Law
1155 East 60th Street
Chicago, IL 60637

The patent laws of the United States are found in Title 35 of the U.S. Code. The seminal grant reads:

Whoever invents or discovers any new and useful process, machine, manufacture, or composition of matter, or any new and useful improvement thereof, may obtain a patent therefor, subject to the conditions and requirements of this Title.

This simple language is the basis for thousands of pages of patent law decisions. However, because of the complexities involved, even these decisions are not the alpha and omega of patent law. Consequently, if you have an invention that you feel might be patentable, you should see a patent attorney. Indeed, patent lawyers are the only subset of the legal profession requiring a separate license in addition to a law degree. Only patent lawyers may prosecute

127

patent applications, although other attorneys may represent patent claimants in patent litigation. Patent agents and, of course, the inventor himself or herself may also prosecute patent applications.

Because of the many difficulties involved, including an uncertainty about under just what circumstances a computer program as part of another invention might be susceptible of patent protection and how much protection would be afforded, patents are seldom sought for computer software. Indeed, to date no patents have been granted for any computer programs standing alone. As will be explained below, software has been the subject of a patent only when it is an integral part of an invention.

PATENT RIGHTS

There are many differences between copyright and patent. As noted above, a patent is a monopoly legally granted to the holder. It is stronger than a copyright in that it covers the idea insofar as the idea is included in the machine or process as well as the expression of the idea. However, like copyright, laws of nature, mathematical formulas, and abstract ideas are not susceptible of protection.

Unlike copyright protection, the independent creation of a patented invention does not prevent the legitimate patentee from keeping the new discoverer from using the invention. The monopoly is absolute. The copyright requirements regarding access and actual copying need not be met to prove patent infringement.

PATENT REQUIREMENTS

It is far more difficult to obtain a patent than a copyright. The procedures are more complex and the basic requirements more stringent. Indeed, individuals are seldom successful without the aid of an attorney. Furthermore, the expenses and long delays render this form of protection more suitable for inventions with a long life expectancy.

While almost all original works can be copyrighted, for a patent to issue there must be considerably more. The invention, process, and so on, must be new and useful and must be a creation that goes beyond the prior art in the field. The invention must also be more than an obvious extension of knowledge generally possessed by the ordinary person skilled in that discipline. This requirement makes it extremely difficult for computer programs to qualify, since the program would have to constitute an invention that is more than an extension of known programming techniques.

Obviously, there are so many different considerations involved that an in-depth discussion of patentability would require another book. Similarly, it is very difficult to state generally what can and can't be patented. Over the years patents have been granted on such diverse items as marijuana pipes, tools, automobile parking structures, valves, drive-in theaters, egg hatchers, game boards, slot machines, and electronic equipment. On the other hand, business forms, perpetual motion machines, promotional advertising schemes, functions, concepts, ideas, algorithms, and laws of nature have all been held to be unpatentable.

COMPUTER PROGRAMS AND PATENTS

Computer programs represent a somewhat unique problem for patent law. As in the case of copyrights, it has been held that laws of nature, physical phenomena, and abstract ideas are excluded from patent protection. Consequently, many authorities have believed that a computer program, which might be considered to be similar to a mathematical formula or algorithm, cannot be the subject of a valid patent. Indeed, the Patent Office examiners regularly refuse patents to computer software standing alone. However, recent decisions by the Supreme Court have indicated that, at least in certain circumstances, software may be subject to patent.

In two cases decided in late 1981, the Court held that a process could be patented, even though a significant part of the process involved the use of a computer system or program.[1] In *Diamond* v. *Diehr,* the Court found patentable a process for transferring uncured synthetic rubber into a different state, allegedly solving certain undercure and overcure problems that had plagued other methods. It had been argued that the computer aspect of the process involved only an algorithm, which was not susceptible of patent protection. However, the Court stressed the entire process as the patentable work and found that the program was just an integral part of that whole work, which was susceptible of patent protection.

Similarly, the outcome of *Diamond* v. *Bradley* was that the design of a particular IC chip was patentable. In that case, the court of appeal held the IC chip to be susceptible of patent protection, even though it contained certain ROM in the design. Again, the Court was looking at the whole and not just the computer program. On appeal, the justices could not agree. Consequently, in light of an equally divided Court, the lower court's ruling remained the law.

These two cases, as well as the numerous comments from the courts that a device is not automatically excluded from patent protection just because a computer is involved, intimate that, at least in some circumstances, computer programs may be patentable. However, these situations appear to be very rare. Indeed, unless the program is an integral part of some other invention, there is still considerable doubt about whether it could be patented alone. Perhaps operating systems, monitors, and other very basic programs that partake more of the machine than the expression of a programmer would be the most likely candidates for patent.

Indeed, in *Apple Computer, Inc., v. Franklin Computer Corp.,* this very issue was raised. Franklin contended that Apple's operating system, monitor, and certain other programs were not susceptible of copyright protection because they are more like machines than expressions. The same argument would tend to favor the availability of patent protection, as opposed to copyright protection, for these works. Although Franklin was initially successful in preventing Apple from obtaining a preliminary injunction, on appeal the reviewing court held that ROM chips could be the subject of a valid copyright and sent the case back to the lower court for reconsideration in light of this ruling.[2] The case then settled leaving the court of appeal decision as the latest expression of law on the subject.

PATENT SEARCHES, FEES, AND DESCRIPTIONS

Besides the higher filing fees ($175.00 minimum), there are several other reasons why attempting to obtain a patent is more costly than copyright. One of the reasons for the high cost of obtaining a patent is the necessity of fully describing in precise detail the invention, how it is made, what it does, and how to use it. There is also usually a description of the prior art.

This refers to the other patented inventions in the same field. The new invention must differ from the old. This is necessary to fulfill the invention requirement of the patent law. To accomplish this, a patent search must be conducted. This is usually handled by companies that specialize in these searches and can be both time-consuming and expensive. However, without this and the services of a patent lawyer, the chances of successfully obtaining a patent are slim.

Of course, there would be very little in the way of prior art for computer programs. After all, except in connection with other products, no patent has actually been issued for any. Still, a search would be required in connection with whatever other process or machine was involved.

COMPLETE DISCLOSURE

Another fundamental problem with patent protection, insofar as computer software is concerned, is the fact that complete disclosure is required. In contrast to trade secret protection, the patent holder must disclose complete details of the invention sufficient to allow another person skilled in the trade to build it. Since mathematical formulas are not susceptible of patent protection, and presumably neither are algorithms, the programmer is faced with the dilemma of having to disclose the very thing he or she is trying to protect. Unlike copyright, the critical code cannot be buried in the center between the first 25 and last 25 pages. It must be wholly set forth and described.

This is even more of a problem when one considers the uncertainty of this form of protection for software. If the issue is ever litigated, the infringer will surely contend that the program was not patentable. This threat is more real than might appear at first. Statistically, most patents that are actually tested through litigation do not hold up. Consequently, in addition to the many uncertainties involved, the would-be software patent holder also faces the probability of not being able to enforce the patent if someone takes him or her to court.

PATENT PROTECTION IMPRACTICAL FOR SOFTWARE

Because of the many problems noted above, it is impractical at this time to consider patent as a viable means of legally protecting computer software. While the courts have insisted that there may be an occasion in which a program standing alone might be patentable, there is so much confusion and uncertainty in the law that it is doubtful that an application would be approved. Furthermore, the costs involved are prohibitive, especially when compared to the modest expenditure involved in copyrighting a program. Therefore, this method of protection cannot be recommended, although if someone were willing to spend the time and money for a legal crusade, there is always a chance that some new law could be made.

NOTES

1. *Diamond* v. *Diehr*, 450 U.S. 175 (1981); and *Diamond* v. *Bradley*, 450 U.S. 381 (1981).

2. *Apple Computer, Inc.*, v. *Franklin Computer Corp.*, 714 F.2d 1240 (3rd Cir. 1983).

20. Trade Secrets

DEFINITION OF A TRADE SECRET

A trade secret is a secret of the trade, comprised of some value and usefulness. A more legalistic definition is found in Section 757 of the Restatement of Torts. The official comment indicates that a trade secret may consist of:

> Any formula, pattern, device, or compilation of information which is used in one's business, and which gives him an opportunity to obtain an advantage over competitors who do not know or use it.

Although trade secret law is found in the state common law, as opposed to a federal statute, virtually all states recognize some form of the above general rule. However, that rule gives precious little guidance, and further elaboration is required to understand the specifics of trade secret protection.

Generally, there are three elements of a trade secret: novelty, secrecy, and value in the trade.

NOVELTY

The novelty requisite to establish a trade secret is far different from that needed to obtain a patent. While a patent requires an invention that extends knowledge beyond the prior art, there is no need for a trade secret to consist of a new discovery or invention. Indeed, sufficient novelty may be found in the particular manner in which generally known principles and concepts are integrated.

133

For example, in creating a data base, different programmers working with basically the same algorithms and knowledge will undoubtedly make different choices regarding how the entire system fits together. If they work independently, the code will certainly not be identical and the differences may result in different interface structures, speed of execution, organization, ease of modification, capacity, and possibly innumerable other differences. Since one of the primary considerations of the law is whether the novelty represents a competitive edge, it has been suggested that virtually all computer software will qualify under this criterion.

COMPUTER PROGRAMS

Some of the other considerations that have been used to justify applying trade secret protection to software include the amount of time and expense dedicated to the development of the trade secret. If the business has devoted a great deal of effort to obtain this competitive advantage, then trade secret protection should be available, assuming the other criteria are met. This is very important in the computer field, where new technology changes daily and even a slight head start on the competition can mean the difference between success and failure.

Although unique combinations or applications of generally known principles might qualify for trade secret protection, generic knowledge does not. Consequently, the knowledge one would learn in the industry anyway cannot be considered a trade secret. This becomes important in the case of noncompetition agreements between employers and employees. These agreements frequently provide that the employee will not use any of the trade secrets of the employer after he or she leaves the job. If such generic knowledge could be considered a trade secret, the programmer would effectively be excluded from the market. On the other hand, a unique application, which meets all of the other qualifications of a trade secret, might be such that the programmer would be prohibited from using or divulging it under this type of agreement. The effects of various programmer–publisher and employer–employee contracts are discussed elsewhere in this book.

VALUE

There is generally little discussion in the case law regarding the requirement that a trade secret must be of value to the user. Probably this is because the mere fact of use demonstrates the value or at least the owner's estimation of such. In connection with computer software, as noted previously, anything that gives one company an edge, even if it only means being first with a particular product by a few months, can be decisive. Consequently, it is fairly safe to assume that any secret worth fighting over will meet the test of value in the trade.

SECRECY

The secrecy requirement is, perhaps, the most important aspect of trade secret law insofar as computer software is concerned. It is also the primary reason why trade secret protection may be very effective in some instances and virtually useless in others.

A trade secret must be kept secret. If it is disclosed generally, the protection is lost. Indeed, even limited disclosures can result in the loss of trade secret protection if no steps are taken to ensure that the person to whom disclosure is made agrees not to further disclose the secret and otherwise to treat the information as a confidential trade secret. There are several different situations in which trade secrets and the secrecy requirement are involved in computer software.

EMPLOYER–EMPLOYEE RELATIONSHIP

Frequently, a company or individual will require the services of another in the course of developing a new product. In the case of software, this might mean hiring a new programmer or seeking a free-lance programmer outside the company. It is quite important to protect the secrets associated with this new development, particularly until the product can be brought to market.

Because confidential information must be divulged in order to allow the new programmer to work on the project, some form of protection is needed to ensure that the employee does not reveal the secret later. This usually takes the form of an agreement or a clause in the employment contract in which the employee agrees not to divulge or use the trade secrets of the employer. For the agreement to be most effective, it should specify as much as possible the nature of the secrets involved. Then, if the employee later misuses those secrets, appropriate action can be taken.

The violation of a nondisclosure agreement will generally not destroy the protectable trade secret nature of the information. Unlike an unprotected voluntary disclosure, when the owner of a trade secret has taken reasonable steps to ensure the privacy of same yet someone else reveals the secret in violation of an express agreement, the secret is not automatically lost. However, the trade secret owner must act to stop the leak and enforce his or her rights once he or she learns of the problem, or such rights may be lost.

LIMITED DISTRIBUTION SOFTWARE

The same considerations and preventive measures that apply in the case of the in-house disclosure of secrets to employees are applicable to the situation in which the software enjoys a limited distribution. Much computer software is written specifically for a particular client or a small group of clients. Until the emergence of the microcomputer, this was probably the way the majority of software purchases were made. A company that needed a particular application program would hire someone to write it. Protection of the trade secrets of the programmer and the company could be handled effectively in a written agreement.

The same is true with respect to software suppliers who have specialized programs for a small segment of the computer user community. Software that is supplied pursuant to a contract is easily handled. The contract can contain all of the necessary statements, precautions, and requirements of nondisclosure adequately to protect the trade secrets. However, this is not true with respect to mass-marketed software.

MASS-MARKETED SOFTWARE

Now that there are more than 2 million personal computers in the marketplace, a broad market for standardized, relatively low-cost, mass-marketed software has developed. This market involves both computer games and business applications. In each case, there are many aspects of the programs involved that the authors or publishers consider constitute trade secrets. Indeed, many people have gone to great lengths in an attempt to prevent others from discovering and using the methods, techniques, and ideas embodied in their software.

Obviously, when thousands of programs are involved, a separately negotiated contract proscribing certain activities for each purchaser or user is impossible. There is simply no way to ensure that everyone will sign a nondisclosure agreement. Consequently, some fairly ingenious methods have been used to attempt to obtain as much protection as possible.

One of the earliest methods involves placing a notice in or on the package or manual supplied with the software limiting the user in what he or she can do to or with the program. Many software purchasers have returned home and discovered, after opening and using the product, a notice in the package that they were not to copy it, show it to anyone, or use it on any machine other than the one it was purchased for (even if they had two computers). Needless to say, most buyers simply ignore these attempted restrictions.

Of even more importance to the one trying to protect the secrets, unless written agreement is obtained from all purchasers, it is unlikely that these kinds of limitations will be enforced or enforceable. There is no way to prove that the purchaser actually saw the limitations or that he or she agreed to them. Further, the classification of the transaction as a sale, as opposed to a license, may create further problems. It is difficult to restrict or control legally what a party does with an object after it has been purchased. Without a signed license agreement, the enforceability of these limitations is questionable at best.

Therefore, it must be assumed that obtaining written agreement from the end user of mass-marketed software is virtually impossible. From a supplier's point of view, it is still a good idea to include limitations on the use of the product. This should be done in a very conspicuous place where it must be seen before purchase and, if possible, on a warranty card that the user will sign and return. However, because of these difficulties, many microcomputer software producers rely more on technical copy protection schemes.

TECHNICAL COPY PROTECTION

One of the most controversial areas of microcomputer software involves the sale of software on disks that are deliberately designed to be difficult, if not impossible, to copy. This usually involves altering the operating system and/or the manner in which information is stored on the disk such that standard copy programs and commands will not work. Although a technical discussion of the methods used is not the purpose of this book, because new methods to foil the other side are found almost daily in this war between the copy protectors and the copiers, anything said is usually obsolete before it is printed.

The software producers who utilize these methods claim that there are more illegal copies of programs than those that are legitimately sold. In the case of inexpensive programs, such as games, where there is no user manual and no need for after-sale support, unless a significant volume of sales can be achieved a publisher will be unable to cover the costs of production and advertising. More expensive business programs may cost several hundred dollars and be subject to hefty royalty payments. Clearly, the publishers are attempting to protect their investments.

On the other hand, those who are dedicated to cracking these protection schemes claim that much software is overpriced and that they should be allowed to make such copies. There are also legitimate needs of users to have backup copies, and many purchasers would also like to learn by reviewing how the programs work. For those with some technical know-how, an unprotected disk can be modified and customized for individual use, while the uncopyable programs cannot. Consequently, breaking into protected disks is considered by some, although not by the law, as a holy war for the consumer.

LEGAL EFFECT OF COPY PROTECTION

While these copy protection schemes may have differing practical effects, the legal effects are not as easily discerned. An argument can be made that—under the theory that the more difficult it is for another to discover your secret from studying your product, the more likely is the availability of trade secret protection—these methods of protection assist in trade secret protection. There are, however, other problems. The general rule of law is that an unprotected disclosure of a trade secret forfeits all legal protection as such. This means that if you supply others with your program without requiring a nondisclosure agreement or some other form of protection, you have lost your trade secret protection.

The fact that the program is protected adds a new wrinkle. As noted, it can be argued that trade secret protection is still available because of the difficulty involved in discovering it. However, the courts have also held that a trade secret will be lost if it can be discovered through study and scrutiny of the product. Therefore, it is possible that a court will find that once the protection method has been broken, the trade secret is lost. (This is a good reason to copyright at least part of the code.)

LOSS BY FAILURE TO ENFORCE

Another problem with trade secret protection is the rule that a party seeking to maintain a trade secret must act to enforce his or her rights thereto. This means that suit must be brought to stop unauthorized disclosures of the secret. In the case of mass-marketed computer software this might be impractical. While it may not be necessary to follow up every sale, once it is learned that some kind of distribution is taking place it seems that some action is called for. The costs of pursuing the pirates might be more than the value of the program, however, thus rendering the sought-after protection too expensive to maintain.

INCOMPATIBILITY WITH COPYRIGHT

While the issue is not totally free from doubt, there are many who believe that trade secret protection is incompatible with copyright. Since copyright requires complete disclosure and trade secret requires secrecy, there are obvious problems involved in attempting to use both to protect the same program. This is not to say that a copyrighted program can't be subject to the copy protection systems used to keep users from making copies of the program. This is perfectly permissible. Of course, a copy of the program is available for public inspection at the Copyright Office in Washington; however, it is questionable whether anyone would bother to hand-copy the program there.

On the other hand, to claim that a program is a trade secret and then deposit a copy for public view with the Copyright Office is somewhat inconsistent. Nevertheless, some courts have indicated that copyright and trade secret are not necessarily mutually exclusive forms of protection and can coexist. A possible way around these difficulties would be to deposit the first 25 pages and the last 25 pages with the Copyright Office and have the most important trade secrets in the middle of the work, which is not deposited. Another suggested method is to use copyright protection for object code and trade secret protection for source code. Then only release the object code to the public. Of course, this would bring registration under the rule of doubt, discussed in earlier chapters, into play.

CONCLUSION

Trade secret protection can be an adjunct to other protection. It can be very powerful in connection with programs that enjoy a very limited distribution where specific agreements can be obtained. It is much less suited to the mass-produced software available for personal computers and probably should be used only in conjunction with other legal forms of protection for these programs.

Part Four

CONTRACTS AND AGREEMENTS

21. Software Publishing Contracts

MANY PROGRAMMERS—FEW PUBLISHERS

Although there are several ways to market computer programs, perhaps the most prevalent in connection with microcomputers is mass marketing through an independent publisher. In fact, the majority of programs for the Apple, IBM, Atari, and Radio Shack personal computers are marketed by a relatively small number of publishing companies, considering the number and variety of the programs. As microcomputers become even bigger business, larger concerns are also entering the software publishing field.

Furthermore, many software designers, both in-house programmers and independents, are contracting with these companies to produce and market their software. The next few chapters will take a look at some of the different types of agreements that can exist between the programmer and the publisher and their various ramifications. In the next chapter, a sample agreement will be discussed in detail, paragraph by paragraph, so that the general discussion in this chapter can be put to practical use.

THE DECISION TO PUBLISH THROUGH ANOTHER

Some programmers wish to keep complete control of all aspects of a product from development through sale to the end user. This almost invariably leads to the establishment of another software house, since the greatest game in the world can't do anything for its creator without publication and promotion. There are thousands of software houses in the United States alone, many of them no more than a room with a computer and an owner with an idea. Some of these will go on to duplicate the success of the two young men who built a microcomputer in a garage and started a small company that ultimately became Apple Computer, Inc.

However, writing a good piece of software and running a publishing house do not necessarily require the same skills. A great programmer is not always a great businessperson. Also, day-to-day business arrangements, such as ordering, marketing, and advertising, require a considerable amount of time. Many programmers would rather be creating their next masterpiece than trying to market their last one. Hence, the need for the publisher/distributor, the software contract, and an attorney.

INITIAL OWNERSHIP

Although the general rule is that the author owns all exclusive rights to a program by virtue of creating it, this is not true in all cases. The most common example is the exception of works for hire, which is discussed in more detail in Chapter 12. The Copyright Act provides that works made for hire are generally the property of the employer. Therefore, the employer, not the author, has the exclusive right to register the copyright to the work.

A work is made for hire when it is prepared by an employee within the scope of his or her employment. For example, if an in-house (employee) programmer is assigned the task of developing a new word processor for the Apple, the rights to that program belong to the employer, not to the employee. If he or she develops the program outside the scope of his or her job, then it belongs to the employee, unless he or she has a different contractual arrangement with the employer. Note that some companies require new employees to sign an agreement stating that all programs conceived or developed while the programmer is employed become the property of the employer, even if such was done outside the office. Whether such an agreement can be enforced depends on the particular circumstances involved.

Additionally, the parties may contractually provide that a certain work is one made for hire in a written agreement. In this situation, however, the work must fall within certain categories, such as contributions, translations, compilations, instructional texts, and supplementary works. Unless the program comes within the exception, it belongs to the author. Furthermore, the Copyright Act provides that the author can transfer rights to the program only by a written agreement. A verbal transfer is ineffectual.

TRANSFERRING OWNERSHIP

There are two primary manners in which a publisher can obtain the rights to your program. First, the publisher may buy it outright. In this case, the publisher becomes the owner of the software, the copyright, and all other rights of ownership.

The publisher may also only be granted a license to market the program. Of course, the rights granted the publisher under a licensing agreement are usually significantly less than under a sale.

To muddy the waters further, sales may be limited to certain parts of the program and licenses may be made subject to innumerable conditions. This chapter will attempt to cover some of the more common provisions found in these arrangements and explain why they are used and which party they are designed to protect. The final agreement, of course, depends on many variables, including the value of the program, the status of the programmer, the standing of the publisher, and the relative skills of the attorneys negotiating the agreement.

SALE OF ALL RIGHTS

Many publishers prefer a transfer or assignment of all rights to a program before they will agree to invest their time, effort, and money in publishing and promoting it. This arrangement lends itself very well to the mass-market microcomputer software industry, particularly in connection with game software. Since the life expectancy for game programs is very short, the sale of exclusive rights seems warranted. However, even the word *all* may have a number of different meanings.

For example, suppose you sell your new game, "Doom Valley," to Superior Software Inc., and the contract provides for the sale of all rights. The game was written for a 48K Apple II Plus. Have you sold the rights to translate the program into TRS–80 format? What about compiling it into machine code? Does the agreement pertain only to sales within the United States or throughout the world? Since these rights can be very valuable, they should be specifically treated in the contract. The failure to reach an agreement can lead to serious problems. However, generally, the sale or transfer of all rights includes all of the rights granted to the author by the copyright laws. Therefore, if this is not what is actually contemplated, something should be done to spell out the rights being transferred more specifically.

OBLIGATIONS OF THE AUTHOR

Another provision commonly contained in these contracts is a noncompetition agreement. In this case, the agreement is usually limited to prohibiting the author from marketing a sequel or competing product for a certain period of time. If the programmer has plans for such a sequel or there is a possibility of such happening, the publisher might be granted the right of first refusal for the next work. This would protect the publisher by requiring the programmer to give the publisher the first opportunity to publish the next program before any other publisher. However, this right would not prevent the programmer from selling it to another if his or her present publisher did not want it. Such provisions must be drafted carefully so each party understands exactly what is required and the procedures that must be followed to comply with the obligations.

In addition to agreeing not to market a competing product for a specified time period, the author will sometimes be requested to agree to assign all enhancements and modifications of the program to the publisher. Depending on the program, this may be with or without additional consideration on the part of the publisher. If significant modifications and enhancements are contemplated that will require much work, such as may be the case with business programs, special provisions should be considered. Of course, the enhancements will presumably increase sales of the product, which will in turn increase the royalty income of the author, so it may sometimes be appropriate to agree to make such enhancements without additional compensation. Again, much depends on the relative strengths of the programmer and the publisher.

The agreement will almost certainly contain a warranty from the author to the publisher that the program is original and that the author has the sole right to copyright the work. It may also include an "indemnity and hold harmless" clause. This section provides that the author will be responsible for any losses suffered by the publisher if anyone challenges the authenticity or copyright that the author is guaranteeing. Although the publisher certainly wants this, the inclusion of the hold harmless language usually means that the author is also responsible for the cost of defense, including attorney's fees, in any action brought by another claiming that the work infringes on his or her rights. Such a hold harmless provision includes responsibility for all costs involved in all litigation, even if the suit is completely frivolous and is later dismissed.

OBLIGATIONS OF THE PUBLISHER

The primary obligation of the publisher is usually to pay the program designer/creator a royalty based on sales of the product. Of course, every programmer wishes to obtain the highest royalty possible. However, what the royalty is based on is just as important as the percentage.

Most royalties are based on actual receipts by the publisher. Since a publisher will usually sell to a distributor at significant discounts (sometimes as much as 50 to 60 percent), a 20 percent royalty on a $30.00 game program may only net the author $2.40 per program. Some publishers may also want to include items such as advertising costs in their expenses, which would further reduce the actual amount received by the programmer. The elements on which the royalty calculation is based should be clearly set out in the contract. Royalties may also be based on other criteria, such as the list price, a percentage of list price, or a flat amount per disk sold.

The publisher may also agree to make an advance against royalties. Of course, the amount will depend on the circumstances. Sometimes the royalty advance is to be paid before the finished program is delivered. The contract should spell out what happens if the program is not completed on time or if the publisher refuses to accept the program. Also, it is possible that even though both the programmer and the publisher are enthusiastic about the product, the public doesn't buy it. In such a situation, the royalties might not even equal the advance. Usually, the author is not required to pay back the advance, but the contract language controls.

Another area of negotiation might be who is responsible for returns. The programmer would like the royalty to be due as soon as the program is shipped from the publisher's warehouse. He or she doesn't want to take the risk of nonpayment by the publisher's customers. He or she also doesn't want to worry about giving back the royalty check if many programs are returned. On the other hand, the publisher may also be unwilling to assume these risks, particularly with an unknown author. This is where a skillful negotiator can make all the difference.

The contract should also contain some basic rights of access to the publisher's records to protect the author. Although the right is seldom used, the programmer should have the right to inspect, at his or her cost and upon reasonable notice, the books and records of the publisher relating to the sale of his or her program. Also, how royalties are to be accounted for and when they are due should be spelled out.

MISCELLANEOUS PROVISIONS

Other miscellaneous provisions that might be incorporated into an agreement include a provision that the parties will execute any additional documents necessary to effectuate the purposes of the agreement, where notices or letters that might be required must be sent, and a provision requiring that the law of a particular state is to be applied to the contract. This last provision is usually inserted so that the attorney who drafted the agreement, and who will presumably be involved in any disputes, can predetermine which law will be applicable. Obviously, it is easier to deal with a problem if you can ensure that the law you are most familiar with will be applied, rather than some other state's law.

LICENSING SOFTWARE FOR PUBLICATION

Virtually all of the same kinds of contract provisions discussed above can also be found in a software license agreement. The primary distinction is that the author does not completely transfer all of his or her rights forever. A license must be for a fixed term. Since the author is not selling his or her rights to the program but merely giving the publisher the right to market and sell the work, the author retains ownership. He or she also usually retains ownership of the copyright but may authorize the licensee to copyright the program in the publisher's name.

Perhaps the single most important aspect of a license is the fact that at the end of the agreement all of the rights revert back to the original owner. This can be advantageous for both parties. For example, after the first year a game program may no longer be a viable product. The publisher does not want to be required to promote the product and may be very happy to allow complete ownership to revert back to the programmer. Also, since the license is for a limited time only, a smaller royalty may be justified. On the other hand, to cover the contingency of a program that becomes a huge success, a license agreement may contain an option to buy out the author's rights for a certain sum. Of course, other hybrid forms of contracts can be devised. The exact form is determined by the requirements and ingenuity of the parties and their attorneys.

Some of the specific differences between sale and license contracts are discussed in the following chapters. While these sample contracts contain many of the provisions discussed herein, they are by no means the only way that these agreements could have been drafted.

22. Specimen Software
Sale Agreement

PRACTICAL EXAMPLES

To further assist in the practical application of this book, a number of sample contracts and documents are supplied as appendices. These contracts and forms may be used as written or customized with appropriate modifications to cover individual needs. It is strongly recommended that an attorney review the final product before signing. In this section, each provision of a sample software author agreement will be discussed. When particular provisions favor one party over the other, special note will be taken.

SALE OR ASSIGNMENT OF ALL RIGHTS

The software author agreement is, in essence, an agreement by the author of a program to transfer all of his or her rights in the program to the publisher in return for the publisher's promise to market the work and pay royalties. Variations of this particular agreement have been used by a number of software publishers in the Apple software market. Additionally, substantially similar provisions will be found in most software publishing agreements. Each section of the sample contract will be discussed separately here.

PARTIES AND PROGRAM

<pre>
                                                    SAA 2-23-83
                    SOFTWARE AUTHOR AGREEMENT

                                    Program Name _____
                                    Computer   _____
     Agreement entered into this ____ day of _____, 198_, by
     and between

                    _____
                    _____
                    _____
                    _____
                                            (Publisher)

                              and

                    _____
                    _____
                    _____
                    _____
              SOC. SEC. #_____
                                            (Author)
</pre>

While this is self-explanatory, it should be noted that this form clearly identifies the "Publisher," "Author," "Program Name," and the type of "Computer" for which the program was written at the very beginning. There is no need to search through numerous pages of text to ascertain these critical details. A good rule to remember in contract drafting is to place all of the changeable elements at the beginning or end, so there will be less likelihood of someone forgetting to fill in a necessary blank. This form requires the completion of the beginning for identification, Appendix A for additions and revisions, and Appendix B for the royalty and any other special terms.

TRANSFER OF ALL RIGHTS

<pre>
     1. The Author hereby sells and assigns to the Publisher all of
     his right, title and interest in and to the software program
     package listed above, said program package consisting of (1) the
     initial diskette or cassette suitable for use with the computer
     listed above and (2) complete program documentation in a form
     suitable for typesetting for use in the User Manual (if any) to be
     provided purchasers of the diskette or cassette, (all of which
     hereinafter is collectively referred to as the "Work").
</pre>

Paragraph 1 provides that the author is transferring all of his or her rights to the program. Obviously, this language benefits the publisher more than the author, but in this case the publisher is paying for the entire work. Note that a reference to the documentation has also been included to avoid any misunderstanding about whether the manual was to be included in the contract.

If someone else will write the manual or the manual is the subject of a separate agreement, these words should be stricken and appropriate language added. If this form is reproduced, one method of accomplishing such a change would be to strike out the offending words physically, initial the changes, and add the new agreement to Appendix B. If the form is retyped, modifications will be easier to make.

Another practical point worthy of note is the definition of *work*. Whenever possible, a good, short definition simplifies drafting and makes the document more readable. It also facilitates editing because a simple change to a definition will carry throughout the contract. However, make sure that is your intention.

DELIVERY DATES AND REVISIONS

```
2.  Author agrees to deliver to the Publisher the completed Work,
including the revisions and additions listed on Appendix A, on or
before the date listed on Appendix A.  Author agrees to make
reasonable revisions to or remedy any defects in the Work within
four weeks of having received written notice of the need for such
revisions or the existence of such defects from Publisher, all of
which revisions or corrections are to be sent to and become the
exclusive property of the Publisher subject to Author's royalty
rights pursuant to the terms hereof.  In the event Author fails or
refuses to make such revisions or remedy such defects, then Pub-
lisher shall have the right to make such revisions or to remedy
such defects and to deduct the costs thereof from any royalties
due the Author pursuant to this Agreement.
```

There should always be a definite date established for the delivery of the work. The first mention of revisions is necessary because of the nature of microcomputer software. Frequently, a publisher will receive a program that is almost finished. It may require a few revisions to be truly marketable. Usually, the publisher and the author will discuss these various issues and how to resolve them. After the publisher has begun working with the author and has assisted in determining what else is needed, he or she should also be protected against the author using one publisher's advice and then going to another at the last minute. Therefore, the contract can be executed and any royalty advance paid at that time. This gives both parties the incentive to cooperate.

The next reference to revisions is necessary from the publisher's point of view because of inevitable program bugs. The section also makes it clear that all revisions come within the scope of the original agreement, and the author is not entitled to additional compensation therefor. Although recognizing his or her imperfections, an author should attempt to set a time limit on program modification. With respect to microcomputer games, their life span is so short that this might not be a problem. However, a business program that may be around for years may present significant difficulties for the programmer who has not looked at the code in two years, even if he or she did originally write it.

Finally, the author may not wish to do such corrective work, or it may be beyond his or her expertise. Since the publisher thought he or she was buying a completed work, it is not unreasonable that any reasonable expenses should be deducted from the author's royalties. Again, a time limit would help clearly to fix the rights of the parties. Also, the obligation of good faith and the "reasonable man" standards, while difficult to define, do set certain guidelines.

PUBLISHER RIGHTS TO SELL AND USE AUTHOR'S NAME

```
3.  Publisher will have the exclusive right to sell the Work
throughout the world to both users and dealers, and all decisions
as to title, sales presentation, trade name, logo and/or other
identification, retail and wholesale prices, and all other matters
of sale, distribution, advertising, and promotion of the Work
shall be in the sole discretion of the Publisher.  Publisher shall
have the right to use the name of the Author for purposes of
advertising and trade in connection with the work and/or any
rights granted hereunder.
```

While the language regarding the publisher's right to market the work is somewhat redundant since all rights were transferred, specifying that matters such as advertising, packaging, and prices are at the sole discretion of the publisher avoids any claim that the work isn't being properly marketed. The author should satisfy himself that the company will do the job he or she wants before signing a contract.

This provision gives the publisher the final word on naming the program. Since the publisher will be responsible for marketing the work, he or she usually wants the right to change, if necessary, the name of the program to one that the publisher feels will sell best. If the program is sold on the condition that a particular name be used, this paragraph must be modified.

It is also a good idea to state specifically whether the right to use the author's name is included in the transfer. The publisher certainly does not want to invade the privacy of the author but may also feel that the author's name will contribute to the marketability of the work. Of course, most programmers want their names included. In fact, some contracts require that the programmer's name be placed prominently on the cover of the product in bold type. Such a requirement could easily be put in Appendix B as:

The author's name shall appear on each page on which the title appears in type larger than all other written matter appearing anywhere on the packaging other than the title.

COMMENCEMENT OF MARKETING

```
4.  Publisher agrees to commence marketing and sale of the Work,
at its own expense not later than 6 months after acceptance by the
Publisher of said Work.  In the event Publisher shall fail to
commence the marketing and sale of the Work within said period or
if Publisher should discontinue the marketing and/or sale of the
Work for 6 consecutive months, then the Author may serve written
demand upon the Publisher, by certified mail, return receipt
requested, requesting the Publisher to commence or continue the
marketing and sale of the Work.  If Publisher shall fail to comply
with such demand within 3 months after receipt of such notice,
then this agreement shall terminate without further notice at the
end of such period.  In the event of termination by the Author
pursuant to this paragraph, such payments as shall have been made
as royalties and/or advances shall be deemed to have been accepted
by Author in full discharge of all of Publisher's obligations to
the Author pursuant to this agreement, and Author shall have no
further claim against Publisher.
```

This paragraph is designed primarily for the protection of the author. If the publisher does not market the program within the designated time or subsequently ceases to market it, the author (by giving written notice) can cause the termination of the agreement and all rights to the work revert back to the author.

The language that such a termination amounts to an acceptance of all royalties previously paid as full settlement for all claims is a bit strong in favor of the publisher although possibly understandable considering the circumstances. This provision allows the publisher to be completely through with the agreement and not to have to worry about it again if the programmer terminates the contract under this paragraph. On the other hand, if there has been a material breach of the contract, it is doubtful that this section would eliminate all other rights.

NONCOMPETITION CLAUSE

While the author spent many difficult hours creating the program, the publisher may spend more time and a great deal of money marketing it. Without

```
5.  Author agrees not to market and/or sell or authorize the
marketing and/or sale of a work which is a sequel to the Work, or
contains characters, shapes, or designs which appear in the Work,
without prior written consent of Publisher.  The Author warrants
that in no event will he publish, market or sell or authorize the
publication, marketing or sale of any other similar or competing
Work of which he is an Author or co-Author until 24 months after
the initiation of the marketing and sale of the Work by Publisher
pursuant hereto, without the prior written consent of Publisher.
```

the requisite advertising and marketing, even the best program can languish. In light of this, few publishers will voluntarily allow an author to capitalize on these promotional activities by selling a sequel or similar work without giving his or her publisher a chance to be involved. Indeed, in the microcomputer field there are a number of programmers who originally worked for one company and, after they achieved a certain amount of success, formed their own companies. While this clause does not prevent that (although it could be designed to do so), it does limit what can be done, at least for a certain time.

REPRESENTATIONS AND INDEMNIFICATION

```
6.  Author warrants and represents that:  (a) The Work is original
and he is the sole Author and proprietor thereof and that the Work
has not been copied, developed or published by any other party;
(b) He has full power and authority to make this agreement and to
grant the rights granted hereunder, and he has not previously
assigned, transferred or otherwise encumbered the same;  (c) The
Work is not in the public domain;  (e) The Work does not infringe
any statutory or common law copyright or any other rights of any
third persons;  (f) The Work does not invade the right of privacy
of any third person, and contains no matter libelous or otherwise
in contravention of the rights of any third person;  (g) The Work
contains no formula or instructions injurious to the user of or
any equipment in which the Work might be utilized.  The warran-
ties, representations and indemnities of the Author herein shall
survive termination of this agreement for any reason.

7.  The Author agrees to indemnify and hold the Publisher harmless
from any damages, including reasonable attorney's fees, in connec-
tion with any claim, action or proceeding inconsistent with or
arising out of a breach of the Author's warranties, representa-
tions and agreements herein contained.  In defending any such
claim, action, or proceeding, Publisher may use counsel of its own
selection.  Publisher shall promptly notify the Author of any such
claim, action or proceeding and the Author shall have the right at
the Author's election to participate in the defense thereof at the
Author's own expense with counsel of the Author's own choosing.
```

The representations in paragraph 6 are for the protection of the publisher but should not present any problem to the legitimate programmer. Paragraph 7 goes a bit further in requiring the author to pick up the tab should anyone claim that the work infringes on another copyright or otherwise violates any of the representations in the preceding paragraph.

Since the expenses involved in defending even a frivolous suit could be considerable, the author should consider whether he or she is receiving enough of a royalty to justify this, should there be any question in his or her mind about a possible adverse claim. It is probably a fair assumption to make that the designers of the Franklin computer anticipated litigation with Apple since they knew they were copying most of Apple's ROM and operating system software. Indeed, in court testimony Franklin admitted to consulting with its attorneys before the sale of its ACE computers. However, most individuals would not have the financial resources of a substantial corporation and would not be in a position to carry such a burden if litigation resulted.

PAYMENT

8. Publisher shall pay to the Author a royalty of the percentage set forth in Appendix B of the Actual Gross Sales from the marketing and sale of the Work. "Actual Gross Sales" shall be the gross amount actually received by Publisher for the sale of copies of the Work, whether at wholesale, retail or otherwise, exclusive of taxes, shipping costs, or other related charges.

9. Publisher shall, within 10 days of the execution of this agreement, mail to Author a check in the amount (if any) set forth in Appendix B as an advance on royalties payable hereunder. The Author's right to royalties and other payments hereunder shall be subject to Publisher's prior right to deduct any and all advances. Author shall not be required to return any portion of any advances if the royalties payable hereunder are less than such advances. However, should Author fail to deliver the Work as provided herein, or fail to meet any obligations hereunder, then such advance shall be forfeited and returned to Publisher within 10 days of written notice of such forfeiture by Publisher to Author.

These paragraphs, with Appendix B, specify the compensation to be received by the author. This is perhaps the most negotiable of all the provisions in the contract. Obviously, the more the publisher wants the program, the more he or she will be willing to pay. A skillful attorney/negotiator can often reap real dividends here, even if he or she receives a portion of the royalty.

Note that the form provides that the advance is to be returned if the author fails to meet his or her obligations. Some contracts provide that once the author delivers the work, the advance is earned, and, even if the program never sells or he or she refuses to do any more work on it, the author does not have to repay the money. On the other hand, the advance could also be treated as a very strict prepayment in anticipation of sales. In such a situation, the contract could provide that any part of the advance not earned within a specified time must be returned. Again, it's up to the parties to the agreement.

ENHANCEMENTS

10. Author covenants to assign all enhancements to the Work developed by him to the Publisher without further or additional consideration or royalty payments. Author acknowledges that all enhancements to the Work, whether developed by him or others, shall become the exclusive property of the Publisher. In the event that Publisher makes payment to any person for enhancements

```
to the Work or has such work performed in-house, which enhance-
ments the Publisher feels are necessary for the successful
marketing and sale of the Work, then the costs of such enhance-
ments shall be deducted from royalties to be paid to the Author
pursuant to this agreement, provided, however, that Author shall
first be given the opportunity by the Publisher to make such
enhancements.
```

This is another negotiable area. While some enhancements seem to be in order, a time limit would help the author in setting a definite time after which he or she will no longer be required to work with the program. Additionally, the language in the form tends to favor the publisher in that it gives the publisher a great deal of discretion. A tighter provision providing only for the correction of program bugs for a limited period of time would be the other side of the coin in favoring the programmer.

TRANSFERRING RIGHTS

```
11.  Publisher shall have the right to sell, assign, license, or
transfer to others any of the rights granted herein to Publisher.
```

While perhaps redundant since all rights have already been assigned, this section makes it clear that the publisher may sell all or part of the rights he or she has purchased. Indeed, this may be beneficial to the programmer in that a small publishing company may transfer the rights to a larger company, which will be in a better position to market the product. On the other hand, if the author wants the transfer to be effective only for the immediate transferee, an express prohibition against transferring these rights should be incorporated into the agreement.

ADAPTATIONS

```
12.  Publisher shall have the right to have the Work adapted
and/or converted to operate on other computer systems other than
the Apple.  Publisher may ask the Author to perform such conver-
sions on a fixed fee basis.  In the event that the Author rejects
such conversion and/or adaptation project, the Author shall have
the right to either: (a) Have the Publisher absorb all expenses
and costs of such conversion and/or adaptation, in which case,
royalties which would have been paid to the Author for the convert-
ed Work shall be retained by the Publisher; or (b) Have the Pub-
lisher's cost of obtaining such conversion or adaptation deducted
from the royalties otherwise payable to him pursuant hereto.  In
```

```
the latter case (b), Author shall be entitled to royalties from
the sale of the converted and/or adapted Work under the same terms
as those for the original Work, after Publisher's costs have been
reimbursed.
```

This can be a very important right and should not be left untreated. Since a program originally designed for one type of computer, particularly in the realm of microcomputer games, will usually not run on another brand of computer, the sale or licensing of the rights to the program should state specifically whether the conversion rights are included. As noted earlier, the rights to convert a program from one language to another or from one dialect of a language to another are contained within the bundle of rights granted by the copyright laws. A transfer of all rights might be construed to assign this right as well, although the failure to include it could certainly lead to misunderstanding.

Since the author may not wish to perform the conversion or may be unable to do so, provisions should be made to allow someone else to handle it. In the form paragraph, two possible scenarios are presented. In the first, the publisher takes the entire risk that the cost for the conversion might exceed revenues on the converted work. Since he or she takes the risk, all royalties go to the publisher. In the second case, the costs of conversion are subtracted from royalties otherwise payable, whether from the original work or from the converted work. Consequently, the programmer receives the same royalties on the converted work after the costs are reimbursed. Of course, he or she also takes the risk that the second version might not sell.

RECORDS AND INSPECTIONS

```
13.  The Publisher shall keep accurate records of all sales of the
Work, and shall render quarterly statements to the Author after
sale and marketing of the Work has been initiated.  Payment of
royalties due to the Author shall be made within three weeks after
the end of the calendar quarter (i.e. March 31, June 30, September
30, and December 31) in which said royalties become due.
```

```
14.  The Author, at his own expense, shall have the right, upon
reasonable notice during usual business hours to examine the books
and records of the Publisher at the place where the same are
regularly maintained insofar as they relate to the Work.
```

These paragraphs, though seldom used and usually unnecessary, assure the author that he or she can check the publisher's books to satisfy himself or herself that royalties are being paid properly. The frequency of payment, of course, may vary without significantly affecting anything else.

ATTORNEY'S FEES

15. Should Publisher employ an attorney to enforce any rights
hereunder, then Author agrees to pay all costs involved therein,
including reasonable attorney's fees in an amount of at least
thirty five percent (35%) of the amount in question or damages
sustained.

This type of provision is seen more and more, primarily because of the high cost of litigation and the fact that the general rule requires each party to pay his or her own attorney fees even if he or she is successful. Since the amounts involved in an infringement action are not always astronomical, a clause such as this adds a little punch to enforcement. A party of dubious integrity who thinks it is not worth the other party's time to sue may think twice before breaching an agreement when he or she sees that, if successful, the suit will not cost his or her opponent anything but will cost himself or herself double. For equality, "Publisher" should be changed to "either party."

ADDITIONAL DOCUMENTS

16. Each party hereto agrees, upon request of the other, to
execute such additional documents as may be reasonably necessary
to confirm the rights of the other party in respect of the Work or
to carry out the intention of this agreement.

Again, such a clause may be superfluous, but it makes it clear that the parties agreed to cooperate in achieving their aims. To this end, each agrees to execute any additional documentation that is required. For example, as noted elsewhere, the Copyright Office might require additional information in connection with the registration of a copyright claim. This clause requires cooperation in filing the additional information requested.

IN-HOUSE PROGRAMMING

17. Publisher shall have the option of performing any programming
work in-house rather than by an outside programmer. In such
event, the value of such work shall be computed at $25.00 per
hour. Publisher shall keep time records or statements thereof
with respect to such work and, upon request, allow reasonable
inspection of same by Author.

If the publisher has the right to perform any programming work in-house for which the author will be charged against royalties (such as debugging or adaptation), a method of valuing the services should be established. Absent such a clause, a court would have to establish a reasonable value. However, such court-determined value may not seem reasonable to the parties.

APPENDIX B REFERENCE

18. Publisher and Author further agree to the additional terms set forth in Appendix B.

This is just an easy way of allowing modifications to the agreement without requiring the retyping of a lot of pages. Just add an appendix.

APPLICABLE LAW

19. This agreement and its interpretation shall be governed by the laws of the State of Louisiana without regard to the choice of law provisions of Louisiana law. Any action to enforce any rights herein shall be brought within the State of Louisiana. This agreement including Appendices A & B, constitutes the entire understanding of the parties concerning the subject matter hereof, and shall not be modified except by a written agreement executed by both parties hereto.

Without a choice of law provision, such as this, there is a possibility of uncertainty about which state law applies. When parties from different states contract and later have a dispute, the applicable law may be that of the state where the last party signed the contract, where the contract was to be performed, where the court interprets that the parties meant, or some other place. Since state laws can differ significantly, it is always a good idea to include such a provision. Since the contracts are usually drafted by the publisher's lawyer, he or she usually chooses his or her state's law.

SIGNATURE BLOCK

IN WITNESS WHEREOF, the parties hereto, referred to herein as Publisher and Author, have executed this agreement as of the day and year first set forth.

_____   _____   _____   _____
    Publisher   DATE   Author   DATE

This section is self-explanatory and, of course, required.

APPENDIX A AND APPENDIX B

<u>APPENDIX A</u>

Author hereby agrees to deliver the completed work ("Work") and to make the listed additions and/or revisions to the Work, which additions and/or revisions shall be delivered with the completed Work, on or before the ____ day of _____, 19__:

Additions and Revisions:

_____   _____   _____   _____
   PUBLISHER   DATE   AUTHOR   DATE

<u>APPENDIX B</u>

In further considerations of the mutual rights and obligations of the foregoing agreement, Author and Publisher agree as follows:

1. The Royalty to be paid to Author shall be _____%.

2. The Royalty advance to Author shall be $_____.

_____   _____   _____   _____
   PUBLISHER   DATE   AUTHOR   DATE

An easy way to incorporate changes without retyping the entire contract is to have appendices such as these. The basic contract refers to the appendices, which contain the terms that will change from work to work.

23. Licensing Agreement

THE DIFFERENCE BETWEEN LICENSE AND SALE

The primary difference between the licensing of a work and the assignment of all rights is the limitation on the time within which the publisher may exercise his or her rights. By definition, a license must be for a fixed time. This may be one year with options to renew, or the license may be for the entire duration of the copyright. The length of the time period is determined by the parties to the agreement, subject only to the limitations of the copyright itself.

Conceptually, the author does not transfer his or her copyright in the program if it is simply made subject to a license granted to a publisher to market the work. However, as a practical matter, the license may contain grants of virtually every right that might be transferred and ultimately be of little difference. As in the sample sale contract, limitations on the publisher's actions can result in the reversion of the program rights back to the author. Thus, a sale contract may, in a sense, be for a limited term like a license. However, the license must always have a definite term.

SPECIMEN PARAGRAPH—LICENSE

Almost all of the language of the specimen sale contract can be used in a license of software rights. Instead of the language relating to the sale of all right, title, and interest to the program, a paragraph similar to the following would be used:

Licensor does hereby grant to Licensee the exclusive license to reproduce, duplicate, copy, market, and offer for sale, at wholesale, retail, or otherwise, by whatever means or medium Licensee deems fit and appropriate at Licensee's sole discretion, the computer program described above.

EXCLUSIVE VS. NONEXCLUSIVE

In the sample language above, the grant was exclusive. Under such a contract, the publisher is the only person allowed to publish the program. It would be improper even for the author to sell or give away copies. A license may also be nonexclusive.

In a nonexclusive license, the owner/author remains at liberty to license others to sell his or her program. Although most microcomputer software publishers would probably want exclusive rights (at least in the United States), there may be instances in which a nonexclusive agreement would be more appropriate. For example, there are several programs for the Apple II computer that are marketed under different names by different publishers.

On a completely different level, much software (including mass-marketed microcomputer software) is technically leased to the ultimate user. That is, the consumer is licensed to use the program under certain circumstances. These licensing arrangements are, of course, nonexclusive in the case of mass-marketed software and most microcomputer software. Otherwise, only one person could use the program. On the other hand, a custom program for a particular company might well be the subject of an exclusive license. (See Chapter 25.)

TERM

As can be readily seen, the only primary difference between the sale and the license agreements is in the expression of the right granted. Of course, as noted above, the license must also be for a specific term. Consequently, a provision such as the one below would also be required in a valid license contract.

TERM OF AGREEMENT: This agreement shall be for an initial term of three years, and shall automatically be renewed for a second term of three years at the expiration of the first three years unless notice of termination is given in accordance with the terms of this agreement.

NOTICE OF TERMINATION: In the event that either party does not wish to renew this agreement, notice of termination and nonrenewal shall be sent to the other party by registered mail, return receipt requested, not less than 60 days before the expiration of the initial term of this agreement. In the absence of such termination, this agreement shall automatically renew in accordance with the terms of this agreement.

OTHER PROVISIONS

Virtually all of the other provisions discussed in Chapter 22 with respect to assignments of all rights may be contained in a license agreement as well. Because of this, a sample agreement will not be duplicated here. However, with the changes noted above, the form contract discussed previously can be used to grant a limited license of certain rights of the copyright holder. Note that sometimes such an agreement is called a royalty agreement. The name is not important. What is important is that it meets the requirements for a valid license.

24. Nondisclosure Agreements

FIRST THINGS FIRST

Before a programmer has to worry about negotiating his or her publishing contract or the manner in which royalties are to be determined, he or she must first find an interested software house (publisher). Only after someone has decided to produce the program do the concerns regarding contract specifics come into play. With the fierce competition in the market, the fears of piracy, and the desire of the programmer to protect his or her investment in time and creativity, the concepts of nondisclosure and secrecy agreements assume new significance.

NO ABSOLUTE CERTAINTY

There is no iron-clad method to guarantee absolutely that someone won't steal an idea once it has been submitted. Indeed, an unscrupulous person could simply lie and say he or she was already working on the same idea. Unless you have the time and money to joust in court and have taken most of the precautions outlined in this book, it is probably not worthwhile to fight. That is, unless you have created the next Visicalc.

As mentioned earlier, ideas (as opposed to the expression of those ideas in, say, a program) cannot be the subject of a valid copyright. Nor can you obtain a patent on them while they are still in their abstract form without being incorporated into an invention. Consequently, a nondisclosure agreement is one of the few written protections available.

THE GOOD FAITH OF THE PUBLISHER

Although this chapter concerns the various methods available for protection and the different elements of a nondisclosure agreement, as a practical matter the good faith of the individuals involved may be far more important than the written agreement. Fortunately, the majority of the larger publishers are honest and have absolutely no intention of stealing a programmer's work. Further, there may actually be a dozen programmers right now working on something similar to what is submitted. Just because a company to which material has been submitted later comes out with something similar does not mean that the idea was somehow misappropriated.

As already noted, an idea is much harder to protect than an actual program. However, following the steps outlined here will reduce the likelihood of misunderstandings and other problems, not to mention strengthening your position in the event of future litigation. The following discussion will also give the freelance programmer a better understanding of the problems facing the publisher. Also, by following these steps, the programmer and the publisher should minimize the chances of misappropriation, whether deliberate or accidental.

REGISTER THE COPYRIGHT FIRST

No program should ever be submitted or shown to anyone without an appropriate copyright notice. (See earlier chapters for a more complete discussion of what is required.) Even though the new Copyright Act is much more lenient than the old law, there is no excuse for not placing the words "Copyright © 1984 by Thorne D. Harris III," with appropriate modifications, on every program you write.

The notice should be incorporated into the program and placed on the label even before it is registered with the Copyright Office and even if you never intend to register it. Registration, as previously noted, gives you additional protection since it establishes the date on which you made an official claim that the material was yours, makes statutory penalties available, and grants certain other procedural rights. Subsequent claims are at a distinct disadvantage. Consequently, it will seldom happen that a program worthy of submission for probable publication is not worthy of spending $10.00 for registration.

PUBLISHER'S RELUCTANCE

Naturally, the programmer would like to have the prospective publisher agree, before inspecting the program, that everything submitted will be considered proprietary trade secrets of the author, and the publisher will not otherwise use any of the ideas, concepts, or code embodied therein or publish anything else similar. However, publishers are understandably reluctant to make such expansive initial agreements. Because other submissions may legitimately contain similar ideas and the added hassle of policing such an agreement with its employees, not to mention the extreme difficulties of proof involved in misappropriation of intellectual property cases, some publishers, to the contrary, require that the author submitting a work agrees to accept the good faith determination of the publisher that it is not independently developing the same program. This is not at all uncommon in the realm of mainframe computer companies.

However, in the micro field the software houses will generally go somewhat further in ensuring protection of the author's submitted information. This is perhaps because of the large number of free-lance authors working with major firms and the fact that the entire industry is still in its infancy. A very large company, on the other hand, would probably be less flexible.

AGREEMENT NOT TO COPY AND TO RETURN SUBMITTED COPIES

This part of the agreement usually presents no problem. Upon submission, the publisher agrees not to copy the work except for copies needed to evaluate the program. Concomitantly, if the decision is made not to accept the program, all materials, including all copies of the program, are either returned to the author or destroyed. Sometimes the publisher requests an archival copy so that he or she has evidence of just what was submitted if any questions arise. While this is not particularly desirable from the author's point of view, such an action also imposes new obligations on the publisher, which he or she may not be willing to undertake.

If the publisher keeps a copy, he or she agrees to continue to keep the author's secrets and take the necessary reasonable steps to ensure such. This means that the publisher must be careful not to inadvertently allow any employees, contract programmers, or even part-time workers to violate the agreement with the author or otherwise improperly copy his or her work. Because of these restrictions and the difficulty of enforcing them, many publishers are agreeable to returning all copies.

It should be remembered, however, that an unsolicited submission is not subject to any specific agreements. Programs not protected by copyright or otherwise should not be sent without some form of agreement to protect the author's rights. The cost of obtaining such protection is small, particularly considering the possible loss. Additionally, since publishers receive many unsolicited programs, they usually will not return them unless they are accompanied by a self-addressed envelope with sufficient postage and a request that the program be returned if the publisher is not interested. (See the step-by-step submission discussion below for further suggestions.)

NOTES, MEMOS, AND RECORDS

The same considerations regarding secrecy and the return of the submission apply with respect to documents generated by the publisher or his or her staff after he or she receives the program. While these evaluation notes actually belong to the publisher, or the staff, they may contain sensitive information about the program. Therefore, the author would like to have them destroyed or turned over to him or her if the program is returned.

Again, there is a conflict. Since the publisher may want to document refusals as well as accepted programs, he or she may wish to keep an archival copy. Clearly, there are conflicting legitimate concerns. One possible solution to this dilemma is to supply the author with a copy of what remains in the file if the publisher wishes to keep a record. In this way, the author will know exactly what is there, and if he or she feels too much is recorded, particular information can be dealt with separately.

TRADE SECRETS

For maximum protection, the author would like a statement from the prospective publisher that the information being submitted is comprised of confidential and proprietary trade secrets of the author and that the publisher will treat them as such. One method of proceeding is first to send a letter requesting agreement to these conditions and only submitting the program after receiving the publisher's signed agreement.

As noted previously, these conditions might place a rather significant burden on the publisher. This is particularly true in connection with programs that others might also be developing. Further, there are so many areas and concepts that would not constitute valid trade secrets that such a blanket statement may not ultimately hold up. Consequently, it is unlikely that such a provision would be necessary in the ordinary submission.

However, there may be certain programs in which the most important element is the concept rather than the actual coding. In these cases the author must walk a narrow line between revealing enough to be enticing to the prospective publisher but not divulging the secret, until an agreement can be reached.

Otherwise, the idea will probably be up for grabs, even though the program is protected through copyright. If the programmer truly feels that such a unique approach is involved and that there is sufficient economic justification, an attorney knowledgeable in this area will be able to tailor an approach that will afford the greatest protection. An example of such conditions that might be incorporated into a first letter is set out below:

AGREEMENT

1. It is understood and agreed that the ideas, concept, designs, plans, and know-how involved in connection with this product are proprietary and confidential information and trade secrets belonging to _____. It is agreed that such information will be treated at all times as confidential and not disclosed to anyone other than the control group necessary to evaluate the idea for marketing purposes. A list of those people to whom the idea is disclosed will be supplied to the undersigned.

2. All notes, data, reference material, sketches, drawings, memoranda documentation, and records in any way incorporating or reflecting any of such confidential information shall belong exclusively to _____ and, unless there is a successful completion of negotiations and transfer of such rights to _____ such information will be delivered to _____ at the conclusion of negotiations.

3. Because of the nature of the confidential information, it is agreed that, in addition to any other remedies available, _____ will be entitled to injunctive relief to enforce the terms of this agreement, since a violation of this agreement would subject her to irreparable injury.

4. It is also agreed that this agreement is made subject to the laws of Louisiana, without respect to the choice of law provisions of Louisiana.

If you agree to these terms, please sign in the space indicated below and return a copy of this letter to the undersigned. We will then forward the information on to you for your evaluation. We thank you for your consideration, and should there be any questions or if you would like to discuss this further, please do not hesitate to call.

Very truly yours,

Thorne D. Harris III

AGREED:

_____

Name:
Title:

Both parties should sign the agreement. It can be placed in a letter, with a line at the bottom for the publisher's signature like the sample, or the agreement may be on a separate document. Of course, the agreement reproduced above strongly favors the author. An example of a nondisclosure agreement that gives greater protection to the publisher is set out on the next page:

NONDISCLOSURE AGREEMENT

You have advised the undersigned that you have a computer program or product and/or idea or concept for one you would like the undersigned to review and evaluate for possible development and/or marketing. We would be pleased to review said product under the following terms:

1. All programs, listings, and other documents submitted by you will be returned to you upon completion of the review if you so request. However, for our records, we may keep one copy of the submission, which will remain in our archives and which will not be released to the general public without your consent.

2. We agree to use reasonable efforts to hold the information delivered by you in confidence. However, because there are many nonprotectable ideas, know-how, and so on, which may be submitted and much material is already in the public domain, and because we frequently receive materials from others which may contain similar ideas and concepts, we can make no warranties or guarantees with respect thereto.

3. We urge you to satisfy yourself of the security and protection of your materials by securing a copyright, or otherwise, and if you have any hesitation, you should not make the submission. We assure you that we will respect all of your valid rights to your materials.

4. We have no intention of misappropriating your ideas and would not remain in business long if we conducted ourselves in that manner. We, therefore, trust you will understand that these terms are designed to protect us both and are necessary because of the nature and complexity of the subject matter.

5. This agreement is to be construed in accordance with the laws of the State of Louisiana without respect to the choice of law provisions of such state, and any action to enforce any provision of this agreement must be brought in Louisiana.

If the above is agreeable to you, please return a signed copy of this letter with your submission.

Program and Material Submitted: _____

Agreed:_____   Sincerely,

Date: _____   _____

While this version of the nondisclosure agreement is considerably different from the earlier one, the basic concepts remain the same. Through negotiation and perhaps by using elements of each agreement, as well as specific language relating to the program in question, an acceptable agreement can be reached.

STEP-BY-STEP SUBMISSION GUIDELINES

The following guidelines are primarily for the programmer and concern the various steps to take in submitting a program to a publisher. While these steps assume the work is for a microcomputer such as an Apple, the basic concepts are applicable to all submissions of intellectual property, not to mention other computer-related uses. It should also be noted that different publishers have different criteria and procedures; however, these general guidelines should still apply.

First, complete the program. This is practical, not legal advice. Unless you have an established relationship with a publisher or are working under contract on a particular project, only finished, debugged programs should ever be submitted. Unfortunately, many submissions are almost finished, which usually means the thing won't run more than halfway through before a major catastrophe occurs. Don't waste your time or the publisher's time, or further submissions may not be given serious consideration.

A letter of inquiry explaining what you have in mind and asking whether the publisher would be interested should be the next step. Although most publishers will review unsolicited materials, by making the inquiry first the programmer can save time and money and avoid publishers who have no interest. You can also request the publisher's standard nondisclosure form or submit your own at this point. Remember, once you have shown someone your confidential information without obtaining their agreement to keep it confidential, you may have lost any effective trade secret protection you had. For major works, or if you are not sure a company will be interested in your program, an inquiry letter should be used.

As noted previously, register the copyright to the program. At least place the copyright notice conspicuously on the label, on the first screen, and in the code. Even without a written nondisclosure agreement this will afford significant protection against unauthorized copying.

Another element often overlooked, particularly by the new programmer, is recordkeeping. Know to whom and when a program is sent. Keep meticulous notes of submissions. If there is no response after four to six weeks, write a followup letter inquiring about the status. If you still don't receive a reply, you should request the return of your materials.

If your program is declined, start the process over with another publisher. Or, perhaps even better, take a look at the program and see if there might not be some enhancements that can be made to improve the chances of acceptance. In any event, if the program is worthwhile, then the effort should be made. A definite lesson can be learned from the two programmers who sent a program for an electronic spread sheet to Apple Computer, Inc., only to be turned down. They decided to market the product themselves, and Visicalc became the all-time best-selling microcomputer program.

25. Warranties, Disclaimers, and Limitations

SALE VS. LEASE

As has been demonstrated, different rights and obligations may arise from the characterization of a software transaction as a sale or a lease. Generally, ownership is maintained in the lease and only specific, designated rights are transferred, while in a sale the ownership in the object itself is transferred, although there may still be limitations on disclosure and copying. Chapters 21, 22, and 23 considered various sale and lease arrangements between the programmer and the publisher. In this chapter some of the duties that arise between the publisher/seller and the purchaser will be treated.

As in the programmer–publisher contracts, when the software is written for one customer or only a small number of users, it is relatively easy to prepare a lease agreement that sets out in detail the rights of all parties. Such a contract would undoubtedly contain specific guarantees regarding exactly what the program is supposed to accomplish. However, mass-marketed software, such as that for personal computers, cannot be easily handled in this manner.

Some companies attempt to license the use of the program by means of a statement on the packaging that says that opening the package constitutes agreement to the terms of the license (usually printed inside). However, more often than not these transactions are considered sales of product. Furthermore, whether sales or licenses, the written agreement of both parties is seldom obtained. How, then, are the rights of the parties determined? What guarantees have actually been made to the purchaser?

EXPRESS AND IMPLIED WARRANTIES

The sale of a product gives rise to certain warranties by the seller that are either express or implied. Express warranties are those to which a company specifically agrees, such as a printed statement that:

Superior Software Inc. guarantees that this program disk will boot on a 48K Apple II Plus, and Superior Software Inc. will replace any defective disk that does not boot or run free of charge.

Although such express agreements may be susceptible of different interpretations and the subject of litigation, they are more explicit than implied warranties. Consequently, the parties usually have a fairly accurate idea of what express warranties have been given.

No one would intentionally spend money on a program, or any other product for that matter, that doesn't work. Although every item sold does not contain an express warranty, the average purchaser does have a reasonable expectation of what the product should do. Therefore, the law has developed the concepts of the implied warranties of merchantability and fitness for the intended use.

DOCTRINE OF MERCHANTABILITY

A product is merchantable and fit if it will pass without objection in the trade and is fit for use for the ordinary purposes for which such goods are generally purchased. Although necessarily dependent on the product in question, these rules provide a basis of protection for the buyer. In connection with computer programs, they would certainly require that the programs perform as advertised or described without significant errors. In other words, the program must not contain errors of such magnitude that the court will reason that a buyer would not have purchased it had he or she known of such.

This test is considered from the viewpoint of the purchaser. If a reasonable person would not have purchased the product with such a defect, then it is not fit. Of course, the nature of computer software and its complexity, as well as the relative lack of sophistication of today's purchasers of mass-produced software, complicate matters. It is impossible to test a program completely in a store for bugs. Indeed, the authors of the program cannot with any certainty say that they have tested all possibilities. Therefore, such authors, publishers, and sellers would like somehow to limit their exposure to problems that might arise after the sale regarding unknown program defects.

DAMAGES

The possibility of being held responsible for damages is a serious consideration for any business involved in selling a product. While the actual purchase price of the individual program is not always significant, it is also possible that the seller would be responsible for consequential damages as a result of a defective product.

Consequential damages are, in this instance, those that arise from the defective program in addition to the program price. For example, if a business has placed all of its inventory and records into an accounting program, becoming totally dependent on it, and the program fails, the entire business will suffer. A $200.00 program may then cause thousands of dollars of damages or more. (This example is expanded on in the next chapter.) If there were no way to limit the seller's exposure to this type of claim, it is probable that fewer companies would enter the market.

DISCLAIMERS AND LIMITATIONS

In an effort to limit exposure, many companies resort to disclaimers and limitations of liability. These are specific notices that should clearly explain what the company selling the product intends the product to do. Unfortunately for the software purchaser, many of the disclaimers that accompany microcomputer software are so expansive that, if taken literally, it is doubtful anyone would buy the product. Consider the following:

DISCLAIMER OF ALL WARRANTIES AND LIABILITY

XXX, Inc., MAKES NO WARRANTIES, EITHER EXPRESS OR IMPLIED, WITH RESPECT TO THIS MANUAL OR WITH RESPECT TO THE SOFTWARE DESCRIBED IN THIS MANUAL, ITS QUALITY, PERFORMANCE, MERCHANTABILITY, OR FITNESS FOR ANY PARTICULAR PURPOSE. XXX, Inc., SOFTWARE IS SOLD OR LICENSED "AS IS." THE ENTIRE RISK AS TO ITS QUALITY AND PERFORMANCE IS WITH THE BUYER. SHOULD THE PROGRAMS PROVE DEFECTIVE FOLLOWING THEIR PURCHASE, THE BUYER (AND NOT XXX, Inc., ITS DISTRIBUTOR, OR ITS RETAILER) ASSUMES THE ENTIRE COST OF ALL NECESSARY SERVICING, REPAIR, OR CORRECTION AND ANY INCIDENTAL OR CONSEQUENTIAL DAMAGES. IN NO EVENT WILL XXX, Inc., BE LIABLE FOR DIRECT, INDIRECT, INCIDENTAL, OR CONSEQUENTIAL DAMAGES RESULTING FROM ANY DEFECT IN THE SOFTWARE, EVEN IF XXX, Inc., HAS BEEN ADVISED OF THE POSSIBILITY OF SUCH DAMAGES. SOME STATES DO NOT ALLOW THE EXCLUSION OR LIMITATION OF IMPLIED WARRANTIES OR LIABILITY FOR INCIDENTAL OR CONSEQUENTIAL DAMAGES, SO THE ABOVE LIMITATION OR EXCLUSION MAY NOT APPLY TO YOU.

Look familiar? The above language is a verbatim quotation from the inside front cover of a manual for a popular software product for the Apple II computer in the $200.00 range. Similar disclaimers can be found with virtually every major business software package for all popular microcomputers.

A cursory glance at this language reveals that the company supplying the product is basically not guaranteeing anything. In fact, this language specifically says that there is no guarantee that the programs will even work. How many users would spend $200.00, or even $20.00, if they really believed that there was a good chance that the program didn't work at all? If it doesn't, does the buyer take all responsibility? Can he or she get a refund? Are these limitations valid?

VALIDITY OF LIMITATIONS

A buyer can, if he or she wants to, buy a program knowing it doesn't work in the hopes of fixing it. It would be unfair later to allow him or her to sue the seller for a refund because the program didn't work. Therefore, the seller must, under certain circumstances, be allowed to limit his or her exposure. If the parties intended to limit liability, then such provisions should be enforced. However, a balancing of the interests of the parties must be made to ascertain whether the limitations will be valid.

Although we must start from the proposition that a contract is the law between the parties and they may contract for virtually anything so long as it is not illegal or immoral, there are several doctrines that have been used to limit exculpatory language such as the example above. These include specific requirements regarding the size and placement of disclaimers on certain products, adequate notice to the buyer, a balancing of the relative bargaining power of each of the parties, and the reasonable expectations of a purchaser. A court weighing these various factors may find that the contract language is unconscionable or contrary to public policy.

Of prime importance to a determination of whether language attempting to limit liability is valid is the issue of whether the buyer was made aware of the limitations before the purchase. For example, the language quoted above was on the inside cover of a manual that came with a sealed software package. It is therefore highly unlikely that a purchaser would have had the opportunity to review this language before opening the box at home. This would tend to make the language unenforceable, although the disclaimer was printed in capital letters on the inside front cover to make it stand out. It is also still an open question about whether the seller would have accepted a return of the product and issued a credit simply because the buyer didn't like the disclaimer.

PROPER NOTICE

In other areas, such as car sales, some jurisdictions require that the disclaimer be somehow brought to the attention of the buyer. This is usually done by having the purchaser sign a notice of disclaimer of warranty, although even this has been held insufficient when it is incorporated into many other papers and would be easily missed by the average person. The same could be done with computer contracts if there are only a few parties to the agreement.

Of course, it is impossible to have every purchaser of a mass-marketed microcomputer program sign such a form. To get around this, some companies place a copy of the disclaimer on the warranty card. The argument is that signing the warranty is also an agreement to waive these rights. However, many users simply don't return the warranty cards. The most effective disclaimers for such computer programs would probably be those placed in a conspicuous place, possibly on the outside of the package, in sufficiently large lettering that it would be virtually impossible for anyone to miss it. To increase the chances of enforceability, other reasonable attempts to give notice, such as those already noted, should also be used.

ADHESION CONTRACTS

Another criterion often considered is the relative bargaining power of the parties. Where one party has a grossly superior position, the courts have refused to uphold certain provisions in favor of that party because the contract was one of adhesion. In these situations, the courts have found that the buyer really had no choice and did not actually agree to the onerous terms of the contract. This is frequently true in connection with form contracts where there is no real bargaining between the parties. Consequently, either the contract or the particular offending provisions are stricken.

In fact, some of the warranty law provisions governing such things as automobile sales are a result of these decisions. Since the cases were not uniform, laws were passed that would allow certain waivers under specific circumstances. Similarly, some states do not allow the same limitations as others. However, the basic concepts discussed here usually still apply.

DOCTRINE OF UNCONSCIONABILITY

These various considerations have also been incorporated into the doctrine of unconscionability. Generally, this rule of law is designed to protect the consumer from oppression and unfair surprise. If the contract is so structured that it simply is not reasonable, a court can refuse to enforce it.

Since business transactions are presumed to be between equals, it is more difficult for a disgruntled buyer of a business program successfully to attack the validity of a software contract. However, the representations of the seller and the reasonable expectations of the buyer, along with the relative bargaining power and sophistication of the parties, will all be considered in reaching a decision on this issue. Since software is usually very complex and the business user may have little or no expertise in the field, he or she is certainly more at the mercy of the seller than he or she would be in other commercial transactions. Hence, an argument can be made that the agreement must be scrutinized for unconscionable limitations.

CONCLUSION

Not all limitations of liability are bad, nor are all such form disclaimers of liability invalid. However, there seems to be a tendency in the computer field to attempt to disclaim all responsibility for a product, even to the extent of claiming the sale is made "as is," without any warranty whatsoever. In many of these situations the doctrine of unconscionability may come to the rescue of the buyer because of attempted overreaching by the seller.

Part Five

MISCELLANEOUS

26. How to Choose a Computer Lawyer

The basics of copyright, patent, trademark, and trade secrets as they relate to computer software have been covered in this book. Obviously, there are times when it is necessary to obtain legal advice from a specialist in these matters, even if no major problems develop. Although much of the filing work does not require an attorney, certain situations do call for special expertise. Additionally, there are a number of ongoing pitfalls that may be encountered in the day-to-day operation of a computer-related business, whether as a programmer, publisher, retailer, or consultant. The prudent businessperson consults a professional for advice in specialized fields.

The early establishment of a good relationship with an attorney who is well equipped to handle computer-related problems will go a long way toward ensuring future success in this business. There are numerous other areas of the law affecting virtually any business in this field that may sometimes require the services of an attorney who understands the intricacies and quirks of the computer industry. The fact that this field is relatively new and changes almost daily makes many otherwise ordinary problems unique when compared to a more traditional business. Consequently, there is a genuine need for an attorney who is familiar with computer law.

A TYPICAL PROBLEM

Consider the following hypothetical problem, which, unfortunately, is not unusual. Dave's Discount Computer Store advertises a full line of personal computers, software, and services, including assistance in setting up small

181

business systems for a moderate fee. Mr. Cosgood, who runs a small insurance agency, wants to buy a personal computer to better handle his insurance accounts and various filing needs. He also wants to learn the rudiments of programming and computers. Dave arranges for Mary, an independent programmer and consultant who frequently assists him in setting up new business systems, to perform an analysis of what the optimum computer/software package for Mr. Cosgood's business would be, given his budget.

After a complete system analysis by Mary, Mr. Cosgood decides to buy his complete system, including a 64K Plum microcomputer, hard and floppy disk drives, printer, financial software, a spread sheet program, and a data base system. All of the hardware and software is purchased from Dave's Discount Computer Store, Dave submits Mary's invoice with his, and Mr. Cosgood pays Dave for everything. Later, Dave reimburses Mary for her work, and Dave does not receive any additional compensation or cut on Mary's work. Dave's Discount Computer Store does not manufacture any of the products it sells. They are all purchased from an out-of-state distributor.

Additionally, being a full-service dealer, Dave provides, through Mary, some slight customization of and setup help with the accounting package and fairly significant extra work with the data base program to meet Mr. Cosgood's needs. In connection with the data base system, Mary spends a number of hours with Mr. Cosgood and his computer, setting up a filing system and explaining to Mr. Cosgood how to operate and further modify it to accomplish his present and anticipated future tasks. Naturally, Mr. Cosgood signs several invoices for products and services, but, except for checking the amount, he does not read the fine print, although there are numerous, specific warranty exclusions, disclaimers, and limitations of liability printed on virtually all of the forms he signs for each product. However, no one specifically points these out to Mr. Cosgood or in any other way calls his attention to them.

Everything works fine for the first three months, and Mr. Cosgood is quite pleased with his new computer. He is so pleased, in fact, that he has taken on a number of new projects and responsibilities without adding to his staff, because the increase in efficiency by using the computer will allow his present staff to handle the additional work. To accomplish this, he spends even more money training his personnel on the use of the system. He also buys a copy of Unlocker, the new super-bit copy program, and makes several unauthorized copies of the programs he procured from Dave with which to attempt a few customizations of his own and for backup purposes. Naturally, he uses the copies and saves the originals in case of emergencies.

At year end, however, when Mr. Cosgood is doing his recap for the year, he discovers that data have been written to the wrong accounts, making all balances useless. Further, there seems to be a bug in the system that causes errors in the addition of four-digit numbers, and negative numbers are ignored. Worse yet, a simple alphabetical sort of his clients takes two hours to complete, before printing! The computer manufacturer has also changed operating systems and no longer supports the one installed in Mr. Cosgood's machine. Although no one will confirm it, there is a rumor that under certain circumstances the old operating system added incorrectly. To add insult to injury, the hard disk drive is full after only three months of data entry, and Mr. Cosgood intended to keep at least two years of accounts on-line at all times. Recreating the lost data and redoing the company books will cost thousands of dollars, far more than the original cost of the entire system. Furthermore, the delays in processing information and correcting errors resulted in Mr. Cosgood's insurance company receiving a bad name in the industry, and his business has greatly diminished.

SORTING OUT RIGHTS AND LIABILITIES

Obviously, there is a distinct possibility that everyone involved in any way with these transactions will be sued, from the computer and peripheral manufacturers to the programmer who assisted in the customization work. There is also an excellent chance that these people will all be pointing the finger at one another. However, the rights and liabilities of each of the parties will depend on a number of contingencies, including the exact nature of each of the transactions (sale of equipment, contract to program, lease or sale of program, etc.) and the written agreements executed by each at the time. The manner and circumstances of signing the contracts, including any verbal promises and warranties made, will also play an important part in determining ultimate liability. Additionally, the reasonable expectations of the parties and the custom and usage in the trade will influence the outcome. Therefore, it makes good sense to consult an attorney familiar with these problems before you find yourself in litigation. Whether you are aligned with the retailer, the programmer, the distributor, or the purchaser, there are a number of things you should be aware of before entering any major transaction.

In the important area of software contracts, for example, there are a number of clauses, such as the disclaimer of warranty and limitation of liability excluding consequential damages (discussed in Chapter 25), which are contained in virtually all of the contracts written for the larger companies, as well as many others. While these provisions may not apply in certain cases, there are strong arguments in favor of including language to delineate clearly the responsibilities of the respective parties and any limitations of liability actually agreed upon. Similarly, the structuring of software agreements as sales or licenses may result in different obligations, liabilities, and time periods within which to assert rights through the initiation of a lawsuit. Clearly, then, there is a need to be able to locate and choose an attorney who is familiar with this subject matter and who will be able to be of real assistance. However, assuming that you recognize the need to consult such a professional before entering into a major undertaking, how do you choose the right attorney?

THE COMPUTER LAWYER

There is no simple answer to the question, "How do I choose a computer lawyer?" There will necessarily be a certain amount of guesswork involved, just as there is in almost any choice. However, there are some basics a nonprofessional should know and certain steps that can be taken to assist in making a reasonable choice. Remember, just as there are numerous programs that accomplish the same objective and you may feel some are more suited to your needs than others, so too will you find many different personalities and abilities in the legal profession. Like software, the fact that you may prefer one method over another does not mean that the other alternative is not any good; it's just different. However, you will be the one who must live with your choice, so you should do what you can to make sure you find an attorney who will be most helpful to you. The information provided in this book should not only give you a basic understanding of the issues involved, but it should also assist in making a decision regarding an attorney to handle these problems.

One immediate and obvious problem is that there is no recognized specialty of computer law. Indeed, there are probably fewer than 75 (some estimates have placed the number closer to 25) attorneys in the country who specialize in computer problems. However, there are other competent attorneys who are not only interested but also knowledgeable about computers and computer law problems in every state. The difficult part is finding them.

Because there are many aspects of computer law that are similar to other areas of the law, some attorneys refuse to accept the concept of computer law as a distinct area. However, there are a number of peculiarities and differences from traditional legal problems that make this field an area where it is quite helpful to know the discipline—computers—as well as the law. Unless the attorney feels comfortable with the subject, there will be an unnecessary tension that must be overcome. Consequently, if you are looking for an attorney to handle your general computer-related problems, it is advisable to find one with as much knowledge of computers and computer law issues as possible.

COMPUTER TERMINOLOGY

What does the attorney know about computers and software? Does he or she understand the terminology and problems you describe? Many attorneys pride themselves on their conservatism and resistance to change. New technologies also intimidate many lawyers, while others simply have no inclination to deal with them. However, familiarity with the subject can be critical.

It is important that the attorney understands, for example, the difference between software and hardware, RAM and ROM, and the other essential terminology that must be mastered before one can effectively counsel in the computer law field. While there is no need for the attorney to be a programmer or computer designer, it is critical that he or she be able to grasp the factual intricacies of the particular situation at hand. This is almost impossible without a basic understanding of the subject matter and a familiarity with the terminology. There is also a practical consideration involved. Since most attorneys charge for their time, if hours must be spent educating the attorney on basic concepts, the overall fee could be considerably higher.

EXPLORE THE SUBJECT

Since your particular problem may involve any number of different situations (such as programmer's contract, sale of software package, royalty agreement or assignment, copyright, trademark, litigation, etc.), you should discuss what you know of the problem with the prospective attorney. Ask how many of these or similar matters he or she has handled in the past. What were the results? Why? How long should it take to bring the matter to a conclusion, and what are your chances of success?

It is also important to realize that it is not absolutely necessary for your attorney to have handled a great number of cases of your particular type. Realistically, since the computer law field is so new, there simply have not been that many precedents. Also, the specific points of law involved will probably have to be researched anyway before the attorney will be able to render an opinion.

Much of an attorney's work is accomplished after the client leaves the office. Just as a programmer may spend many hours on a program that is not extremely long, the lawyer must research the latest law, determine what your best course of action will be, and formulate some sort of plan. Legal research alone can be extremely time-consuming, and it can sometimes take hours to find the one case that resolves an issue. Nonetheless, this background work is essential if you are to prevail. On the other hand, the attorney's knowledge and experience in this field is an important factor, since it is likely that you will end up paying extra to educate your lawyer if he or she must learn about computers in addition to researching a specific legal point.

MAKING FIRST CONTACT

Unfortunately, the yellow pages do not contain a heading entry for "Computer Lawyers." However, there are several methods to simplify the search.

First, many local bar associations have referral services that assist clients in locating an attorney. Usually, the initial consultation fee is low, thus allowing an inexpensive interview before a commitment is made. Because of the newness of the area, it is unlikely that there will be a category of computer lawyers in the referral directory. However, there may be references to copyright, contract, litigation, or the other related issues involved. Also, the referral service may know of an attorney involved with computers and software.

Another source of information is the American Bar Association. There are several "sections," which are really subgroups, within the ABA that are involved with computers and software. For example, the Copyright, Trademark, and Patent section and the section on Law, Science, and Technology both contain many members with experience in these fields. By contacting the local ABA office or the main office in Chicago, a lead or two might be developed, although the ABA is not a referral service.

If you already have an attorney, he or she should be able to make a few of these inquiries to determine which colleague you can consult. It may take some effort to find someone, but it should be worth the trouble.

ATTORNEY'S FEES

The fee to be charged is often a gray area that causes many clients and attorneys unnecessary embarrassment. This is unfortunate and can be easily remedied. No one has ever had any hesitation in asking the price of a computer! Likewise, you should not have any second thoughts about discussing your lawyer's fee. After all, you expect to pay any professional who performs a service for you, whether he or she is a doctor, a plumber, or an attorney.

There are two basic types of fee arrangements used in connection with legal services. First, your attorney can charge on an hourly basis. This arrangement would be most likely if you engaged a lawyer for general advice, to review or draft a contract, or to render a legal opinion on your exposure in a certain circumstance. Also, most defense work (when you have been sued rather than when you are the one suing) is handled on an hourly basis. The advantages to this include being able to keep better track of the costs as you go, provided you agree on periodic billings rather than one billing at conclusion, and paying a fixed amount for work actually performed.

Hourly rates differ greatly. However, just because one attorney's rate is less than another's does not necessarily mean he or she will cost less in the long run. An experienced attorney may charge much more than another who is less familiar with computer law. However, he or she may be able to accomplish the same result in much less time, actually costing less overall. The attorney's familiarity with the subject matter can be as important as his or her familiarity with the law.

The other major fee arrangement calls for the attorney to share in the recovery, if any. This sort of contingency fee is the primary form of compensation in personal injury cases. It allows a plantiff, who can't afford to pay as he or she goes, to hire a lawyer to press his or her claim. The attorney does not receive any fee unless he or she wins, in which case the lawyer gets a percentage (usually from 30 to 50 percent) of the amount the client would have received. Obviously, in cases where there are serious injuries or other significant monetary damages, the successful attorney will receive far more than he or she would have on an hourly arrangement. Some copyright and patent infringement litigation is also done on a contingency basis, and there is no prohibition to making such an agreement in other instances.

Other possible fee arrangements include a set cost for a particular service, such as $100.00 to prepare, process, and file a copyright. If a fixed fee can be set, you will know exactly what your costs will be. However, this may be impossible unless your needs are very specific. You could also agree to transfer part of a royalty as payment for services. This might allow the poor, starving programmer the opportunity to obtain legal assistance at little or no out-of-pocket cost. Later, if the programmer's work becomes the success he or she hopes it will be, the attorney will share in the proceeds, if not the glory. This would be very similar to a contingency fee, although it may partake a little of partnership as well.

SUMMARY

The important thing to remember is not to be timid about asking questions. Ask about the lawyer's knowledge of computers, ask about experience, and ask about fees. Computer law is a new field, and there are no established rules to show the way clearly. By taking an active part in the initial contacts and discussing these issues thoroughly with your attorney, you can not only find the assistance you need but also help shape this new area of the law.

27. A Little Philosophy

OVERVIEW OF PROTECTION

In this book I have attempted to give an overview of the different methods available to legally protect computer software. While almost all of the legal methods that can be used have been in existence for years, they are being adapted with considerable success to this new technology. Additionally, there are continuing studies regarding the possibility of creating new forms of protection for software or further modifying present rules to better handle some of the unique aspects of computer programs.

Additionally, the computer industry itself, and particularly the rapidly expanding microcomputer field, is developing new means of physical or mechanical protection every day. These methods usually employ a modified operating system such that it is not only very difficult to copy the disk, but it is also almost impossible to modify or view the program. These limitations have caused many users to complain.

Purchasers want to be able to make a backup copy of important disks to avoid catastrophes if something should go wrong. Furthermore, many of the users of microcomputer software are hobbyists who want to be able to tinker with the program. By studying how others have accomplished a particular task and modifying their programs to suit additional needs, the purchaser is afforded one of the greatest learning experiences available in this field. Consequently, to counter the physical protection schemes being developed to prevent access to programs, a subindustry devoted to cracking these codes has arisen, and progress in this field is advancing as rapidly as in the other.

As a dramatic example, when work on this book was begun, the nibble or bit copy programs appeared to be the most sophisticated method by which unauthorized copies of microcomputer programs for the Apple II were made. However, during the course of preparing the manuscript, a number of hardware copy products have become available to copy so-called protected Apple programs. These plug-in peripheral boards apparently allow almost anyone to copy any program in memory.

NEED FOR PROTECTION

There is clearly a need to protect the time and money spent by the author, the publisher, and the seller of computer software. One of the truisms about software is that, while a good program is hard to write and requires a great deal of effort to do properly, it is generally very easy to copy.

As programs become more sophisticated and require hundreds or thousands of man-hours to develop and market, this inherent ability to make copies becomes a limiting factor. If others can easily make unauthorized copies of the program, the developers may never recoup their development costs. If that happens on a widespread basis, development of quality microcomputer software will cease because of unprofitability, which would be disastrous for the entire industry. Consequently, it is easy to understand why publishers do everything possible to prevent users from being able to copy the programs, even if such protection schemes limit the usability and versatility of the program itself.

However, the nature of the microcomputer industry must also be considered. Since many of the users are hobbyists and others who legitimately need or want to be able to get into the program without any thought of violating anyone's rights, a conflict arises. Unfortunately, this conflict has not been resolved.

MIXED EMOTIONS

Obviously, the need to protect the author's work is real. However, by locking up the program in such a manner that the purchaser cannot learn from or modify it, a disservice to many may occur. Furthermore, since there are means available to break virtually every method of protection, the ones who really lose are the honest users who would not buy the code-breaking programs or peripherals but who would like to learn from or modify the program.

Although it is not a perfect solution, I would prefer more emphasis on legal protection and less on mechanical protection as a means of accomplishing all goals. Certainly, the legal means are present, and new laws designed to further protect programmers are in the offing. Although it might not be practical to sue an individual who makes one illegal copy for a friend, there are certainly incentives to prosecute the pirate who distributes many copies of the product illegally.

Physical copy protection could then be limited to those programs for which it was absolutely essential. Additionally, other means might be employed to minimize unauthorized copying and ensure a fair return on the programmer's and publisher's investment. For example, incentives not to copy, such as free updates and additional services, could be available only to registered owners, or the right to copy could be granted for a small additional fee, or perhaps even some amount of advertising on the disk could help defray costs.

It is hoped that the industry will mature to such an extent that these problems will diminish and all concerned will benefit. Regardless, the principles discussed in this book will still be valid. For the author or owner to legally protect his or her work while maximizing its usefulness is ultimately the best system for all.

APPENDICES

Appendix A

FORM TX

UNITED STATES COPYRIGHT OFFICE

REGISTRATION NUMBER
TX   TXU
EFFECTIVE DATE OF REGISTRATION
Month   Day   Year

DO NOT WRITE ABOVE THIS LINE. IF YOU NEED MORE SPACE, USE CONTINUATION SHEET (FORM TX/CON)

① Title

TITLE OF THIS WORK:

PREVIOUS OR ALTERNATIVE TITLES:

If a periodical or serial give: Vol. ...... No. ...... Issue Date ....

PUBLICATION AS A CONTRIBUTION: (If this work was published as a contribution to a periodical, serial, or collection, give information about the collective work in which the contribution appeared.)

Title of Collective Work .... Vol. ...... No. ...... Date .... Pages ....

② Author(s)

IMPORTANT: Under the law, the "author" of a "work made for hire" is generally the employer, not the employee (see instructions). If any part of this work was "made for hire" check "Yes" in the space provided, give the employer (or other person for whom the work was prepared) as "Author" of that part, and leave the space for dates blank.

1

NAME OF AUTHOR:

Was this author's contribution to the work a "work made for hire"? Yes ...... No ......

DATES OF BIRTH AND DEATH:
Born .... Died ....
(Year)   (Year)

AUTHOR'S NATIONALITY OR DOMICILE:
Citizen of .... { or } Domiciled in ....
(Name of Country)   (Name of Country)

WAS THIS AUTHOR'S CONTRIBUTION TO THE WORK:
Anonymous? Yes ...... No ......
Pseudonymous? Yes ...... No ......
If the answer to either of these questions is "Yes," see detailed instructions attached.

AUTHOR OF: (Briefly describe nature of this author's contribution)

2

NAME OF AUTHOR:

Was this author's contribution to the work a "work made for hire"? Yes ...... No ......

DATES OF BIRTH AND DEATH:
Born .... Died ....
(Year)   (Year)

AUTHOR'S NATIONALITY OR DOMICILE:
Citizen of .... { or } Domiciled in ....
(Name of Country)   (Name of Country)

WAS THIS AUTHOR'S CONTRIBUTION TO THE WORK:
Anonymous? Yes ...... No ......
Pseudonymous? Yes ...... No ......
If the answer to either of these questions is "Yes," see detailed instructions attached.

AUTHOR OF: (Briefly describe nature of this author's contribution)

3

NAME OF AUTHOR:

Was this author's contribution to the work a "work made for hire"? Yes ...... No ......

DATES OF BIRTH AND DEATH:
Born .... Died ....
(Year)   (Year)

AUTHOR'S NATIONALITY OR DOMICILE:
Citizen of .... { or } Domiciled in ....
(Name of Country)   (Name of Country)

WAS THIS AUTHOR'S CONTRIBUTION TO THE WORK:
Anonymous? Yes ...... No ......
Pseudonymous? Yes ...... No ......
If the answer to either of these questions is "Yes," see detailed instructions attached.

AUTHOR OF: (Briefly describe nature of this author's contribution)

③ Creation and Publication

YEAR IN WHICH CREATION OF THIS WORK WAS COMPLETED:

Year ....
(This information must be given in all cases.)

DATE AND NATION OF FIRST PUBLICATION:

Date ....
(Month)   (Day)   (Year)

Nation ....
(Name of Country)
(Complete this block ONLY if this work has been published.)

④ Claimant(s)

NAME(S) AND ADDRESS(ES) OF COPYRIGHT CLAIMANT(S):

TRANSFER: (If the copyright claimant(s) named here in space 4 are different from the author(s) named in space 2, give a brief statement of how the claimant(s) obtained ownership of the copyright.)

- Complete all applicable spaces (numbers 5-11) on the reverse side of this page
- Follow detailed instructions attached   • Sign the form at line 10

DO NOT WRITE HERE
Page 1 of .... pages

195

EXAMINED BY:	APPLICATION RECEIVED:	
CHECKED BY:		FOR COPYRIGHT OFFICE USE ONLY
CORRESPONDENCE: ☐ Yes	DEPOSIT RECEIVED:	
DEPOSIT ACCOUNT FUNDS USED: ☐	REMITTANCE NUMBER AND DATE:	

DO NOT WRITE ABOVE THIS LINE. IF YOU NEED ADDITIONAL SPACE, USE CONTINUATION SHEET (FORM TX/CON)

PREVIOUS REGISTRATION:

- Has registration for this work, or for an earlier version of this work, already been made in the Copyright Office?   Yes ....   No ....
- If your answer is "Yes," why is another registration being sought? (Check appropriate box)
  - ☐ This is the first published edition of a work previously registered in unpublished form.
  - ☐ This is the first application submitted by this author as copyright claimant.
  - ☐ This is a changed version of the work, as shown by line 6 of this application.
- If your answer is "Yes," give: Previous Registration Number .... Year of Registration ....

(5) Previous Registration

COMPILATION OR DERIVATIVE WORK: (See instructions)

PREEXISTING MATERIAL: (Identify any preexisting work or works that this work is based on or incorporates.)

{ ....

MATERIAL ADDED TO THIS WORK: (Give a brief, general statement of the material that has been added to this work and in which copyright is claimed.)

{ ....

(6) Compilation or Derivative Work

MANUFACTURERS AND LOCATIONS: (If this is a published work consisting preponderantly of nondramatic literary material in English, the law may require that the copies be manufactured in the United States or Canada for full protection. If so, the names of the manufacturers who performed certain processes, and the places where these processes were performed must be given. See instructions for details.)

NAMES OF MANUFACTURERS	PLACES OF MANUFACTURE
....	....
....	....
....	....

(7) Manufacturing

REPRODUCTION FOR USE OF BLIND OR PHYSICALLY-HANDICAPPED PERSONS: (See instructions)

- Signature of this form at space 10, and a check in one of the boxes here in space 8, constitutes a non-exclusive grant of permission to the Library of Congress to reproduce and distribute solely for the blind and physically handicapped and under the conditions and limitations prescribed by the regulations of the Copyright Office: (1) copies of the work identified in space 1 of this application in Braille (or similar tactile symbols); or (2) phonorecords embodying a fixation of a reading of that work; or (3) both.

  a ☐ Copies and phonorecords   b ☐ Copies Only   c ☐ Phonorecords Only

(8) License For Handicapped

DEPOSIT ACCOUNT: (If the registration fee is to be charged to a Deposit Account established in the Copyright Office, give name and number of Account.)

Name: ....

Account Number: ....

CORRESPONDENCE: (Give name and address to which correspondence about this application should be sent.)

Name: ....
Address: ....
                                          (Apt.)
       (City)   (State)   (ZIP)

(9) Fee and Correspondence

CERTIFICATION: ✱ I, the undersigned, hereby certify that I am the: (Check one)

☐ author ☐ other copyright claimant ☐ owner of exclusive right(s) ☐ authorized agent of: ....
                                                              (Name of author or other copyright claimant, or owner of exclusive right(s))

of the work identified in this application and that the statements made by me in this application are correct to the best of my knowledge.

☞   Handwritten signature: (X) ....

Typed or printed name: ....   Date ....

(10) Certification (Application must be signed)

MAIL CERTIFICATE TO

.... (Name)
.... (Number, Street and Apartment Number)
.... (City)   (State)   (ZIP code)

(Certificate will be mailed in window envelope)

(11) Address For Return of Certificate

✱ 17 U.S.C. § 506(e): Any person who knowingly makes a false representation of a material fact in the application for copyright registration provided for by section 409, or in any written statement filed in connection with the application, shall be fined not more than $2,500.

☆ U.S. GOVERNMENT PRINTING OFFICE: 1980: 311-425/3

Jan. 1980—500,000

Appendix B

FORM VA
UNITED STATES COPYRIGHT OFFICE

REGISTRATION NUMBER
VA   VAU

EFFECTIVE DATE OF REGISTRATION

(Month)   (Day)   (Year)

DO NOT WRITE ABOVE THIS LINE. IF YOU NEED MORE SPACE, USE CONTINUATION SHEET (FORM VA/CON)

1
Title

TITLE OF THIS WORK:

NATURE OF THIS WORK: (See instructions)

Previous or Alternative Titles

PUBLICATION AS A CONTRIBUTION: (If this work was published as a contribution to a periodical, serial, or collection, give information about the collective work in which the contribution appeared.)

Title of Collective Work   Vol   No   Date   Pages

2
Author(s)

IMPORTANT: Under the law, the "author" of a "work made for hire" is generally the employer, not the employee (see instructions). If any part of this work was "made for hire" check "Yes" in the space provided, give the employer (or other person for whom the work was prepared) as "Author" of that part, and leave the space for dates blank.

1

NAME OF AUTHOR:

DATES OF BIRTH AND DEATH:
Born _____ (Year)   Died _____ (Year)

Was this author's contribution to the work a "work made for hire"?   Yes   No

AUTHOR'S NATIONALITY OR DOMICILE:
Citizen of _____ (Name of Country) } or { Domiciled in _____ (Name of Country)

WAS THIS AUTHOR'S CONTRIBUTION TO THE WORK:
Anonymous?   Yes   No
Pseudonymous?   Yes   No

AUTHOR OF: (Briefly describe nature of this author's contribution)

If the answer to either of these questions is "Yes," see detailed instructions attached

2

NAME OF AUTHOR:

DATES OF BIRTH AND DEATH:
Born _____ (Year)   Died _____ (Year)

Was this author's contribution to the work a "work made for hire"?   Yes   No

AUTHOR'S NATIONALITY OR DOMICILE:
Citizen of _____ (Name of Country) } or { Domiciled in _____ (Name of Country)

WAS THIS AUTHOR'S CONTRIBUTION TO THE WORK:
Anonymous?   Yes   No
Pseudonymous?   Yes   No

AUTHOR OF: (Briefly describe nature of this author's contribution)

If the answer to either of these questions is "Yes," see detailed instructions attached

3

NAME OF AUTHOR:

DATES OF BIRTH AND DEATH:
Born _____ (Year)   Died _____ (Year)

Was this author's contribution to the work a "work made for hire"?   Yes   No

AUTHOR'S NATIONALITY OR DOMICILE:
Citizen of _____ (Name of Country) } or { Domiciled in _____ (Name of Country)

WAS THIS AUTHOR'S CONTRIBUTION TO THE WORK:
Anonymous?   Yes   No
Pseudonymous?   Yes   No

AUTHOR OF: (Briefly describe nature of this author's contribution)

If the answer to either of these questions is "Yes," see detailed instructions attached

3
Creation and Publication

YEAR IN WHICH CREATION OF THIS WORK WAS COMPLETED:

Year _____

(This information must be given in all cases.)

DATE AND NATION OF FIRST PUBLICATION:

Date _____ (Month)   (Day)   (Year)

Nation _____ (Name of Country)

(Complete this block ONLY if this work has been published.)

4
Claimant(s)

NAME(S) AND ADDRESS(ES) OF COPYRIGHT CLAIMANT(S):

TRANSFER: (If the copyright claimant(s) named here in space 4 are different from the author(s) named in space 2, give a brief statement of how the claimant(s) obtained ownership of the copyright.)

- Complete all applicable spaces (numbers 5-9) on the reverse side of this page
- Follow detailed instructions attached   • Sign the form at line 8

DO NOT WRITE HERE
Page 1 of _____ pages

197

	EXAMINED BY:	APPLICATION RECEIVED:	FOR COPYRIGHT OFFICE USE ONLY
	CHECKED BY:		
	CORRESPONDENCE: ☐ Yes	DEPOSIT RECEIVED:	
	DEPOSIT ACCOUNT FUNDS USED: ☐	REMITTANCE NUMBER AND DATE:	

DO NOT WRITE ABOVE THIS LINE. IF YOU NEED ADDITIONAL SPACE, USE CONTINUATION SHEET (FORM PA/CON)

PREVIOUS REGISTRATION:

⑤
Previous Registration

- Has registration for this work, or for an earlier version of this work, already been made in the Copyright Office? Yes . . . . No . . . .

- If your answer is "Yes," why is another registration being sought? (Check appropriate box)

    ☐ This is the first published edition of a work previously registered in unpublished form.

    ☐ This is the first application submitted by this author as copyright claimant.

    ☐ This is a changed version of the work, as shown by line 6 of the application.

- If your answer is "Yes," give: Previous Registration Number . . . . Year of Registration . . . .

COMPILATION OR DERIVATIVE WORK: (See instructions)

⑥
Compilation or Derivative Work

PREEXISTING MATERIAL: (Identify any preexisting work or works that the work is based on or incorporates.)

. . . .

. . . .

. . . .

MATERIAL ADDED TO THIS WORK: (Give a brief, general statement of the material that has been added to this work and in which copyright is claimed.)

. . . .

. . . .

. . . .

DEPOSIT ACCOUNT: (If the registration fee is to be charged to a Deposit Account established in the Copyright Office, give name and number of Account.)

Name: . . . .

Account Number: . . . .

CORRESPONDENCE: (Give name and address to which correspondence about this application should be sent.)

Name: . . . .

Address: . . . .
                                                                       (Apt.)

. . . .
(City)   (State)   (ZIP)

⑦
Fee and Correspondence

CERTIFICATION: ✱ I, the undersigned, hereby certify that I am the: (Check one)

☐ author ☐ other copyright claimant ☐ owner of exclusive right(s) ☐ authorized agent of . . . .
                                                                                                              (Name of author or other copyright claimant, or owner of exclusive right(s))

of the work identified in this application and that the statements made by me in this application are correct to the best of my knowledge.

Handwritten signature: (X) . . . .

Typed or printed name . . . . Date . . . .

⑧
Certification
(Application must be signed)

. . . .
                                          (Name)

. . . .
                          (Number, Street and Apartment Number)

. . . .
        (City)   (State)   (ZIP code)

MAIL CERTIFICATE TO

(Certificate will be mailed in window envelope)

⑨
Address For Return of Certificate

✱ 17 U.S.C. §506(e) FALSE REPRESENTATION—Any person who knowingly makes a false representation of a material fact in the application for copyright registration provided for by section 409, or in any written statement filed in connection with the application, shall be fined not more than $2,500.

☆ U.S. GOVERNMENT PRINTING OFFICE: 1980-311-425/11

Aug. 1980—150,000

Appendix C

FORM PA

UNITED STATES COPYRIGHT OFFICE

REGISTRATION NUMBER
PA   PAU
EFFECTIVE DATE OF REGISTRATION
....
(Month)   (Day)   (Year)

DO NOT WRITE ABOVE THIS LINE. IF YOU NEED MORE SPACE, USE CONTINUATION SHEET (FORM PA/CON)

① Title

TITLE OF THIS WORK:

NATURE OF THIS WORK: (See instructions)

PREVIOUS OR ALTERNATIVE TITLES:

② Author(s)

IMPORTANT: Under the law, the "author" of a "work made for hire" is generally the employer, not the employee (see instructions). If any part of this work was "made for hire" check "Yes" in the space provided, give the employer (or other person for whom the work was prepared) as "Author" of that part, and leave the space for dates blank.

1

NAME OF AUTHOR:

Was this author's contribution to the work a "work made for hire"?   Yes......   No......

DATES OF BIRTH AND DEATH:
Born........ Died........
(Year)   (Year)

AUTHOR'S NATIONALITY OR DOMICILE:
Citizen of .... } or { Domiciled in ....
(Name of Country)   (Name of Country)

WAS THIS AUTHOR'S CONTRIBUTION TO THE WORK:
Anonymous?   Yes......   No......
Pseudonymous?   Yes......   No......
If the answer to either of these questions is "Yes," see detailed instructions attached.

AUTHOR OF: (Briefly describe nature of this author's contribution)

2

NAME OF AUTHOR:

Was this author's contribution to the work a "work made for hire"?   Yes......   No......

DATES OF BIRTH AND DEATH:
Born........ Died........
(Year)   (Year)

AUTHOR'S NATIONALITY OR DOMICILE:
Citizen of .... } or { Domiciled in ....
(Name of Country)   (Name of Country)

WAS THIS AUTHOR'S CONTRIBUTION TO THE WORK:
Anonymous?   Yes......   No......
Pseudonymous?   Yes......   No......
If the answer to either of these questions is "Yes," see detailed instructions attached.

AUTHOR OF: (Briefly describe nature of this author's contribution)

3

NAME OF AUTHOR:

Was this author's contribution to the work a "work made for hire"?   Yes......   No......

DATES OF BIRTH AND DEATH:
Born........ Died........
(Year)   (Year)

AUTHOR'S NATIONALITY OR DOMICILE:
Citizen of .... } or { Domiciled in ....
(Name of Country)   (Name of Country)

WAS THIS AUTHOR'S CONTRIBUTION TO THE WORK:
Anonymous?   Yes......   No......
Pseudonymous?   Yes......   No......
If the answer to either of these questions is "Yes," see detailed instructions attached.

AUTHOR OF: (Briefly describe nature of this author's contribution)

③ Creation and Publication

YEAR IN WHICH CREATION OF THIS WORK WAS COMPLETED:
Year..........
(This information must be given in all cases.)

DATE AND NATION OF FIRST PUBLICATION:
Date........
(Month)   (Day)   (Year)
Nation........
(Name of Country)
(Complete this block ONLY if this work has been published.)

④ Claimant(s)

NAME(S) AND ADDRESS(ES) OF COPYRIGHT CLAIMANT(S):

TRANSFER: (If the copyright claimant(s) named here in space 4 are different from the author(s) named in space 2, give a brief statement of how the claimant(s) obtained ownership of the copyright.)

• Complete all applicable spaces (numbers 5-9) on the reverse side of this page
• Follow detailed instructions attached   • Sign the form at line 8

DO NOT WRITE HERE
Page 1 of .... pages

EXAMINED BY	APPLICATION RECEIVED	
CHECKED BY		FOR COPYRIGHT OFFICE USE ONLY
CORRESPONDENCE ☐ Yes	DEPOSIT RECEIVED	
DEPOSIT ACCOUNT FUNDS USED ☐	REMITTANCE NUMBER AND DATE	

DO NOT WRITE ABOVE THIS LINE. IF YOU NEED ADDITIONAL SPACE, USE CONTINUATION SHEET (FORM VA/CON)

PREVIOUS REGISTRATION:

- Has registration for this work, or for an earlier version of this work, already been made in the Copyright Office? Yes .... No ....

- If your answer is "Yes," why is another registration being sought? (Check appropriate box)
  ☐ This is the first published edition of a work previously registered in unpublished form.
  ☐ This is the first application submitted by this author as copyright claimant.
  ☐ This is a changed version of the work, as shown by line 6 of the application.

- If your answer is "Yes," give: Previous Registration Number .... Year of Registration ....

⑤ Previous Registration

COMPILATION OR DERIVATIVE WORK: (See instructions)

PREEXISTING MATERIAL: (Identify any preexisting work or works that this work is based on or incorporates.)

....
....
....

MATERIAL ADDED TO THIS WORK: (Give a brief, general statement of the material that has been added to this work and in which copyright is claimed.)

....
....
....

⑥ Compilation or Derivative Work

DEPOSIT ACCOUNT: (If the registration fee is to be charged to a Deposit Account established in the Copyright Office, give name and number of Account.)

Name ....

Account Number ....

CORRESPONDENCE: (Give name and address to which correspondence about this application should be sent.)

Name ....

Address .... (Apt.)

(City) .... (State) .... (ZIP) ....

⑦ Fee and Correspondence

CERTIFICATION: ✱ I, the undersigned, hereby certify that I am the: (Check one)
☐ author ☐ other copyright claimant ☐ owner of exclusive right(s) ☐ authorized agent of ....
(Name of author or other copyright claimant, or owner of exclusive right(s))
of the work identified in this application and that the statements made by me in this application are correct to the best of my knowledge.

Handwritten signature: (X) ....

Typed or printed name .... Date ....

⑧ Certification (Application must be signed)

MAIL CERTIFICATE TO

.... (Name)
.... (Number, Street and Apartment Number)
.... (City) .... (State) ...... (ZIP code)

(Certificate will be mailed in window envelope)

⑨ Address For Return of Certificate

Appendix D

FORM CA
UNITED STATES COPYRIGHT OFFICE

REGISTRATION NUMBER

TX	TXU	PA	PAU	VA	VAU	SR	SRU	RE

Effective Date of Supplementary Registration

....
(MONTH)   (DAY)   (YEAR)

DO NOT WRITE ABOVE THIS LINE. FOR COPYRIGHT OFFICE USE ONLY

Ⓐ
Basic Instructions

TITLE OF WORK:

REGISTRATION NUMBER OF BASIC REGISTRATION:

YEAR OF BASIC REGISTRATION:

NAME(S) OF AUTHOR(S):

NAME(S) OF COPYRIGHT CLAIMANT(S):

Ⓑ
Correction

LOCATION AND NATURE OF INCORRECT INFORMATION IN BASIC REGISTRATION:

Line Number . . . . Line Heading or Description . . . .

INCORRECT INFORMATION AS IT APPEARS IN BASIC REGISTRATION:

CORRECTED INFORMATION:

EXPLANATION OF CORRECTION: (Optional)

Ⓒ
Amplification

LOCATION AND NATURE OF INFORMATION IN BASIC REGISTRATION TO BE AMPLIFIED:

Line Number . . . . Line Heading or Description . . . .

AMPLIFIED INFORMATION:

EXPLANATION OF AMPLIFIED INFORMATION: (Optional)

		FORM CA RECEIVED:	FOR COPYRIGHT OFFICE USE ONLY
	EXAMINED BY: .... CHECKED BY:		
	CORRESPONDENCE: ☐ YES	REMITTANCE NUMBER AND DATE:	
	REFERENCE TO THIS REGISTRATION ADDED TO BASIC REGISTRATION: ☐ YES ☐ NO	DEPOSIT ACCOUNT FUNDS USED: ☐	

DO NOT WRITE ABOVE THIS LINE. FOR COPYRIGHT OFFICE USE ONLY

CONTINUATION OF: (Check which) ☐ PART B OR ☐ PART C

Ⓓ Continuation

DEPOSIT ACCOUNT: If the registration fee is to be charged to a Deposit Account established in the Copyright Office, give name and number of Account:

Name .... Account Number ....

Ⓔ Deposit Account and Mailing Instructions

CORRESPONDENCE: Give name and address to which correspondence should be sent:

Name .... Apt. No. ....

Address ....
      (Number and Street)   (City)   (State)   (ZIP Code)

CERTIFICATION ✱ I, the undersigned, hereby certify that I am the: (Check one)

☐ author ☐ other copyright claimant ☐ owner of exclusive right(s) ☐ authorized agent of: ....
                                                                              (Name of author or other copyright claimant, or owner of exclusive right(s))

of the work identified in this application and that the statements made by me in this application are correct to the best of my knowledge.

Ⓕ Certification (Application must be signed)

Handwritten signature: (X) ....

Typed or printed name: ....

Date: ....

✱ 17 USC §506(e): FALSE REPRESENTATION—Any person who knowingly makes a false representation of a material fact in the application for copyright registration provided for by section 409, or in any written statement filed in connection with the application, shall be fined not more than $2,500.

MAIL CERTIFICATE TO

....
                              (Name)
....
                (Number, Street and Apartment Number)
....
      (City)   (State)   (ZIP code)

(Certificate will be mailed in window envelope)

Ⓖ Address for Return of Certificate

U.S. GOVERNMENT PRINTING OFFICE: 1978—261-822/11   Apr. 1978—250,000

Appendix E

FORM RE

UNITED STATES COPYRIGHT OFFICE

REGISTRATION NUMBER

EFFECTIVE DATE OF RENEWAL REGISTRATION

....
(Month)   (Day)   (Year)

DO NOT WRITE ABOVE THIS LINE.   FOR COPYRIGHT OFFICE USE ONLY

① Renewal Claimant(s)

RENEWAL CLAIMANT(S), ADDRESS(ES), AND STATEMENT OF CLAIM: (See Instructions)

1
Name ....
Address ....
Claiming as ....
(Use appropriate statement from instructions)

2
Name ....
Address ....
Claiming as ....
(Use appropriate statement from instructions)

3
Name ....
Address ....
Claiming as ....
(Use appropriate statement from instructions)

② Work Renewed

TITLE OF WORK IN WHICH RENEWAL IS CLAIMED:

RENEWABLE MATTER:

CONTRIBUTION TO PERIODICAL OR COMPOSITE WORK:
Title of periodical or composite work: ....
If a periodical or other serial, give: Vol .... No. .... Issue Date ....

③ Author(s)

AUTHOR(S) OF RENEWABLE MATTER:

④ Facts of Original Registration

ORIGINAL REGISTRATION NUMBER:
....

ORIGINAL COPYRIGHT CLAIMANT:

ORIGINAL DATE OF COPYRIGHT:
• If the original registration for this work was made in published form, give: OR   • If the original registration for this work was made in unpublished form, give:

DATE OF PUBLICATION: ....
(Month)   (Day)   (Year)

DATE OF REGISTRATION: ....
(Month)   (Day)   (Year)

203

EXAMINED BY:	RENEWAL APPLICATION RECEIVED:	FOR
CHECKED BY:		COPYRIGHT
DEPOSIT ACCOUNT FUNDS USED: ☐	REMITTANCE NUMBER AND DATE:	OFFICE USE ONLY

DO NOT WRITE ABOVE THIS LINE. FOR COPYRIGHT OFFICE USE ONLY

RENEWAL FOR GROUP OF WORKS BY SAME AUTHOR: To make a single registration for a group of works by the same individual author published as contributions to periodicals (see instructions), give full information about each contribution. If more space is needed, request continuation sheet (Form RE/CON).

⑤
Renewal for Group of Works

1
Title of Contribution: ....
Title of Periodical: .... Vol. ...... No. ...... Issue Date ....
Date of Publication: .... Registration Number: ....
(Month)   (Day)   (Year)

2
Title of Contribution: ....
Title of Periodical: .... Vol. ...... No. ...... Issue Date ....
Date of Publication: .... Registration Number: ....
(Month)   (Day)   (Year)

3
Title of Contribution: ....
Title of Periodical: .... Vol. ...... No. ...... Issue Date ....
Date of Publication: .... Registration Number: ....
(Month)   (Day)   (Year)

4
Title of Contribution: ....
Title of Periodical: .... Vol. ...... No. ...... Issue Date ....
Date of Publication: .... Registration Number: ....
(Month)   (Day)   (Year)

5
Title of Contribution: ....
Title of Periodical: .... Vol. ...... No. ...... Issue Date ....
Date of Publication: .... Registration Number: ....
(Month)   (Day)   (Year)

6
Title of Contribution: ....
Title of Periodical: .... Vol. ...... No. ...... Issue Date ....
Date of Publication: .... Registration Number: ....
(Month)   (Day)   (Year)

7
Title of Contribution: ....
Title of Periodical: .... Vol. ...... No. ...... Issue Date ....
Date of Publication: .... Registration Number: ....
(Month)   (Day)   (Year)

DEPOSIT ACCOUNT: (If the registration fee is to be charged to a Deposit Account established in the Copyright Office, give name and number of Account.)

Name: ....
Account Number: ....

CORRESPONDENCE: (Give name and address to which correspondence about this application should be sent.)

Name: ....
Address: ....
(Apt.)
....
(City)   (State)   (ZIP)

⑥
Fee and Correspondence

CERTIFICATION: I, the undersigned, hereby certify that I am the: (Check one)
☐ renewal claimant   ☐ duly authorized agent of: ....
(Name of renewal claimant)
of the work identified in this application, and that the statements made by me in this application are correct to the best of my knowledge.

☞ Handwritten signature: (X) ....
Typed or printed name: ....
Date: ....

⑦
Certification (Application must be signed)

MAIL CERTIFICATE TO
....
(Name)
....
(Number, Street and Apartment Number)
....
(City)   (State)   (ZIP code)

MAIL CERTIFICATE TO
(Certificate will be mailed in window envelope)

⑧
Address for Return of Certificate

Appendix F

| TRADEMARK APPLICATION, PRINCIPAL REGISTER, WITH DECLARATION (Individual) | MARK (identify the mark) |
| | CLASS NO. (if known) |

TO THE COMMISSIONER OF PATENTS AND TRADEMARKS:

NAME OF APPLICANT, AND BUSINESS TRADE NAME, IF ANY

BUSINESS ADDRESS

RESIDENCE ADDRESS

CITIZENSHIP OF APPLICANT

The above identified applicant has adopted and is using the trademark shown in the accompanying drawing[1] for the following goods: _____

_____ ,

and requests that said mark be registered in the United States Patent and Trademark Office on the Principal Register established by the Act of July 5, 1946.

The trademark was first used on the goods[2] on _____ ; was first used on the goods[2] in
_____ (date)

_____ commerce[3] on _____ ;
(type of commerce) *(date)*
and is now in use in such commerce.

4

The mark is used by applying it to[5] _____

_____

and five specimens showing the mark as actually used are presented herewith.

6

_____ .
(name of applicant)
being hereby warned that willful false statements and the like so made are punishable by fine or imprisonment. or both, under Section 1001 of Title 18 of the United States Code and that such willful false statements may jeopardize the validity of the application or any registration resulting therefrom, declares that he/she believes himself/herself to be the owner of the trademark sought to be registered; to the best of his/her knowledge and belief no other person. firm, corporation, or association has the right to use said mark in commerce, either in the identical form or in such near resemblance thereto as may be likely, when applied to the goods of such other person, to cause confusion, or to cause mistake, or to deceive; the facts set forth in this application are true; and all statements made of his/her own knowledge are true and all statements made on information and belief are believed to be true.

_____
(signature of applicant)

_____
(date)

Form PTO - 1476 (Rev. 10-82) *(Instructions on reverse side)*   Patent and Trademark Office - U.S. DEPT. of COMMERCE

Appendix G

<table>
<tr>
<td rowspan="2">TRADEMARK APPLICATION, PRINCIPAL
REGISTER, WITH DECLARATION
(Partnership)</td>
<td>MARK (identify the mark)</td>
</tr>
<tr>
<td>CLASS NO. (if known)</td>
</tr>
</table>

TO THE COMMISSIONER OF PATENTS AND TRADEMARKS:

NAME OF PARTNERSHIP

NAMES OF PARTNERS

BUSINESS ADDRESS OF PARTNERSHIP

CITIZENSHIP OF PARTNERS

The above identified applicant has adopted and is using the trademark shown in the accompanying drawing[1] for the following goods: _____

_____ ,

and requests that said mark be registered in the United States Patent and Trademark Office on the Principal Register established by the Act of July 5, 1946.

The trademark was first used on the goods[2] on _____ ; was first used on the goods[2] in
_____ (date)
_____ commerce[3] on _____ ; and is now in use in
(type of commerce)   (date)
such commerce.

4

The mark is used by applying it to[5] _____

_____

and five specimens showing the mark as actually used are presented herewith.

6

_____ ,
(name of partner)

being hereby warned that willful false statements and the like so made are punishable by fine or imprisonment, or both, under Section 1001 of Title 18 of the United States Code and that such willful false statements may jeopardize the validity of the application or any registration resulting therefrom, declares that he/she is a partner of applicant partnership; he/she believes said partnership to be the owner of the trademark sought to be registered; to the best of his/her knowledge and belief no other person, firm, corporation, or association has the right to use said mark in commerce, either in the identical form or in such near resemblance thereto as may be likely, when applied to the goods of such other person, to cause confusion, or to cause mistake, or to deceive; the facts set forth in this application are true; and all statements made of his/her own knowledge are true and all statements made on information and belief are believed to be true.

_____
(signature of partner)

_____
(date)

Form PTO - 1477 (4 - 82)   (Instructions on reverse side)   Patent and Trademark Office - U.S. DEPT. of COMMERCE

Appendix H

Form PTO 1478 (Rev. 10-82) (Instructions on reverse side)   Patent and Trademark Office - U.S. DEPT. of COMMERCE

TRADEMARK APPLICATION, PRINCIPAL REGISTER, WITH DECLARATION (Corporation)	MARK (identify the mark)
	CLASS NO. (if known)

TO THE COMMISSIONER OF PATENTS AND TRADEMARKS:

NAME OF CORPORATION 1

STATE OR COUNTRY OF INCORPORATION

BUSINESS ADDRESS OF CORPORATION

The above identified applicant has adopted and is using the trademark shown in the accompanying drawing[2] for the following goods: _____

_____ ,

and requests that said mark be registered in the United States Patent and Trademark Office on the Principal Register established by the Act of July 5, 1946.

The trademark was first used on the goods[3] on _____ ; was first used on the goods[3] in
_____ (date)

_____ commerce[4] on _____ ; and is now in use in
(type of commerce)   (date)

such commerce.

5

The mark is used by applying it to[6] _____

_____

and five specimens showing the mark as actually used are presented herewith.

7

_____ ,
(name of officer of corporation)

being hereby warned that willful false statements and the like so made are punishable by fine or imprisonment, or both, under Section 1001 of Title 18 of the United States Code and that such willful false statements may jeopardize the validity of the application or any registration resulting therefrom, declares that he/she is

_____
(official title)

of applicant corporation and is authorized to execute this instrument on behalf of said corporation; he/she believes said corporation to be the owner of the trademark sought to be registered; to the best of his/her knowledge and belief no other person, firm, corporation, or association has the right to use said mark in commerce, either in the identical form or in such near resemblance thereto as may be likely, when applied to the goods of such other person, to cause confusion, or to cause mistake, or to deceive; the facts set forth in this application are true; and all statements made of his/her own knowledge are true and all statements made on information and belief are believed to be true.

_____
(name of corporation)

By _____
(signature of officer of corporation, and official title of officer)

_____
(date)

207

Appendix I

Prepared and Furnished by
JAMES H. "JIM" BROWN
Secretary of State

STATE OF LOUISIANA
SECRETARY OF STATE
BATON ROUGE, LOUISIANA

**APPLICATION TO REGISTER TRADE-MARKS
AND TRADE-NAMES OR SERVICE MARKS**

Corporations Division
P. O. Box 44125
Baton Rouge, LA 70804
Phone No. (504) 925-4701

Pursuant to Revised Statutes of 1950, Title 51, Chapter 1, Part VI, as amended, relating to the registration,
renewal, use and protection of trade-marks and trade-names or service marks.

This application may be used by an individual, firm, corporation, association, union or other organization and is to be
completed and submitted to the Secretary of State in original form only.

Application must be accompanied by check or money order in the amount of $10.00 per application made payable to the
Secretary of State. Be sure to answer all questions on the form.

Refer To The Reverse Side Of This Form For General Instructions For Filing Application And For Classification.

CHECK ONE: ☐ TRADE-MARK ☐ TRADE-NAME ☐ SERVICE MARK
Identifies A Product / Idenfifies A Business / Identifies A Service

CHECK ONE: ☐ ORIGINAL FILING ☐ RENEWAL

1
Name Of Person(s) Or Corporation Applying For Registration

Full Street Address And/Or P. O. Box, City, State And Zip Code Of Applicant

If Applicant Is A Corporation, List State Of Incorporation

2
Name Of Trade-Mark, Trade-Name, Or Service Mark Applied For By Applicant. If A Logo Is Included, Please Describe.

3
List the Goods, Services, Or Type Of Business To Which The Name Or Mark Is Applied

4
Classification Number (Separate Form for Each Class) See Reverse Side Of Form
ENTER CLASS NUMBER HERE:

5
State The Manner In Which The Mark Or Name Is Used In Connection With Specific Goods, Services, Or Type Of Business

6
Date Mark Or Name Was First Used By Applicant Or Predecessor*
Month & Day , 19 Year

Date Mark Or Name Was First used In Louisiana*
Month & Day , 19 Year

*
The Mark Or Name Must Be In Use On The Date Of This Application. Reservations Are Available For Names Not Yet In Use.
(See Reverse Side, General Instruction No. 6)

7
If The Logo Of Your Mark Or Name Is Part Of Your Registration , Attach Three (3) Copies Of Your Logo (Design, Artwork, Sketch, etc.) here:

AFFIDAVIT

8
STATE

PARISH OR COUNTY

I, the applicant am the owner of the mark or name sought to be registered and no other person, firm, association, union or
corporation has the right to such use in such class, either in the identical form hereinabove described, or in any such
resemblance thereto as may be calculated to deceive, and the facsimiles or counterparts herewith filed are true and
correct.

NAME OF APPLICANT

AUTHORIZED PERSON

TITLE

Sworn to and subscribed before me, this _____ day

of _____, 19 ____

The above named person, by his signature, swears that he is the applicant, or an
authorized representative of the applicant, named in the foregoing application, and
that the facts alleged in said application are true.

NOTARY PUBLIC   APPLICANT OR AUTHORIZED REPRESENTATIVE

208

Appendix J

SAA 2-23-83

SOFTWARE AUTHOR AGREEMENT

Program Name _____
Computer   _____

Agreement entered into this _____ day of _____, 198_, by and between

_____
_____
_____
_____
                                    (Publisher)

                    and

_____
_____
_____
_____
SOC. SEC. # _____
                                    (Author)

1. The Author hereby sells and assigns to the Publisher all of his right, title and interest in and to the software program package listed above, said program package consisting of (1) the initial diskette or cassette suitable for use with the computer listed above and (2) complete program documentation in a form suitable for typesetting for use in the User Manual (if any) to be provided purchasers of the diskette or cassette, (all of which hereinafter is collectively referred to as the "Work").

2. Author agrees to deliver to the Publisher the completed Work, including the revisions and additions listed on Appendix A, on or before the date listed on Appendix A. Author agrees to make reasonable revisions to or remedy any defects in the Work within four weeks of having received written notice of the need for such revisions or the existence of such defects from Publisher, all of which revisions or corrections are to be sent to and become the exclusive property of the Publisher subject to Author's royalty rights pursuant to the terms hereof. In the event Author fails or refuses to make such revisions or remedy such defects, then Publisher shall have the right to make such revisions or to remedy such defects and to deduct the costs thereof from any royalties due the Author pursuant to this Agreement.

3. Publisher will have the exclusive right to sell the Work throughout the world to both users and dealers, and all decisions as to title, sales presentation, trade name, logo and/or other identification, retail and wholesale prices, and all other matters of sale, distribution, advertising, and promotion of the Work shall be in the sole discretion of the Publisher. Publisher shall have the right to use the name of the Author for purposes of advertising and trade in connection with the work and/or any rights granted hereunder.

4. Publisher agrees to commence marketing and sale of the Work, at its own expense not later than 6 months after acceptance by the

Publisher of said Work. In the event Publisher shall fail to
commence the marketing and sale of the Work within said period or
if Publisher should discontinue the marketing and/or sale of the
Work for 6 consecutive months, then the Author may serve written
demand upon the Publisher, by certified mail, return receipt
requested, requesting the Publisher to commence or continue the
marketing and sale of the Work. If Publisher shall fail to comply
with such demand within 3 months after receipt of such notice,
then this agreement shall terminate without further notice at the
end of such period. In the event of termination by the Author
pursuant to this paragraph, such payments as shall have been made
as royalties and/or advances shall be deemed to have been accepted
by Author in full discharge of all of Publisher's obligations to
the Author pursuant to this agreement, and Author shall have no
further claim against Publisher.

5. Author agrees not to market and/or sell or authorize the
marketing and/or sale of a work which is a sequel to the Work, or
contains characters, shapes, or designs which appear in the Work,
without prior written consent of Publisher. The Author warrants
that in no event will he publish, market or sell or authorize the
publication, marketing or sale of any other similar or competing
Work of which he is an Author or co-Author until 24 months after
the initiation of the marketing and sale of the Work by Publisher
pursuant hereto, without the prior written consent of Publisher.

6. Author warrants and represents that: (a) The Work is original
and he is the sole Author and proprietor thereof and that the Work
has not been copied, developed or published by any other party;
(b) He has full power and authority to make this agreement and to
grant the rights granted hereunder, and he has not previously
assigned, transferred or otherwise encumbered the same; (c) The
Work is not in the public domain; (e) The Work does not infringe
any statutory or common law copyright or any other rights of any
third persons; (f) The Work does not invade the right of privacy
of any third person, and contains no matter libelous or otherwise
in contravention of the rights of any third person; (g) The Work
contains no formula or instructions injurious to the user of or
any equipment in which the Work might be utilized. The warranties, representations and indemnities of the Author herein shall
survive termination of this agreement for any reason.

7. The Author agrees to indemnify and hold the Publisher harmless
from any damages, including reasonable attorney's fees, in connection with any claim, action or proceeding inconsistent with or
arising out of a breach of the Author's warranties, representations and agreements herein contained. In defending any such
claim, action, or proceeding, Publisher may use counsel of its own
selection. Publisher shall promptly notify the Author of any such
claim, action or proceeding and the Author shall have the right at
the Author's election to participate in the defense thereof at the
Author's own expense with counsel of the Author's own choosing.

8. Publisher shall pay to the Author a royalty of the percentage
set forth in Appendix B of the Actual Gross Sales from the marketing and sale of the Work. "Actual Gross Sales" shall be the gross

amount actually received by Publisher for the sale of copies of
the Work, whether at wholesale, retail or otherwise, exclusive of
taxes, shipping costs, or other related charges.

9.   Publisher shall, within 10 days of the execution of this
agreement, mail to Author a check in the amount (if any) set forth
in Appendix B as an advance on royalties payable hereunder. The
Author's right to royalties and other payments hereunder shall be
subject to Publisher's prior right to deduct any and all advances.
Author shall not be required to return any portion of any advances
if the royalties payable hereunder are less than such advances.
However, should Author fail to deliver the Work as provided
herein, or fail to meet any obligations hereunder, then such
advance shall be forfeited and returned to Publisher within 10
days of written notice of such forfeiture by Publisher to Author.

10.   Author covenants to assign all enhancements to the Work
developed by him to the Publisher without further or additional
consideration or royalty payments. Author acknowledges that all
enhancements to the Work, whether developed by him or others,
shall become the exclusive property of the Publisher. In the
event that Publisher makes payment to any person for enhancements
to the Work or has such work performed in-house, which enhancements the Publisher feels are necessary for the successful
marketing and sale of the Work, then the costs of such enhancements shall be deducted from royalties to be paid to the Author
pursuant to this agreement, provided, however, that Author shall
first be given the opportunity by the Publisher to make such
enhancements.

11.   Publisher shall have the right to sell, assign, license, or
transfer to others any of the rights granted herein to Publisher.

12.   Publisher shall have the right to have the Work adapted
and/or converted to operate on other computer systems other than
the Apple. Publisher may ask the Author to perform such conver-
sions on a fixed fee basis. In the event that the Author rejects
such conversion and/or adaptation project, the Author shall have
the right to either: (a) Have the Publisher absorb all expenses
and costs of such conversion and/or adaptation, in which case,
royalties which would have been paid to the Author for the converted Work shall be retained by the Publisher; or (b) Have the Publisher's cost of obtaining such conversion or adaptation deducted
from the royalties otherwise payable to him pursuant hereto. In
the latter case (b), Author shall be entitled to royalties from
the sale of the converted and/or adapted Work under the same terms
as those for the original Work, after Publisher's costs have been
reimbursed.

13.   The Publisher shall keep accurate records of all sales of the
Work, and shall render quarterly statements to the Author after
sale and marketing of the Work has been initiated. Payment of
royalties due to the Author shall be made within three weeks after
the end of the calendar quarter (i.e. March 31, June 30, September
30, and December 31) in which said royalties become due.

14. The Author, at his own expense, shall have the right, upon reasonable notice during usual business hours to examine the books and records of the Publisher at the place where the same are regularly maintained insofar as they relate to the Work.

15. Should Publisher employ an attorney to enforce any rights hereunder, then Author agrees to pay all costs involved therein, including reasonable attorney's fees in an amount of at least thirty five percent (35%) of the amount in question or damages sustained.

16. Each party hereto agrees, upon request of the other, to execute such additional documents as may be reasonably necessary to confirm the rights of the other party in respect of the Work or to carry out the intention of this agreement.

17. Publisher shall have the option of performing any programming work in-house rather than by an outside programmer. In such event, the value of such work shall be computed at $25.00 per hour. Publisher shall keep time records or statements thereof with respect to such work and, upon request, allow reasonable inspection of same by Author.

18. Publisher and Author further agree to the additional terms set forth in Appendix B.

19. This agreement and its interpretation shall be governed by the laws of the State of Louisiana without regard to the choice of law provisions of Louisiana law. Any action to enforce any rights herein shall be brought within the State of Louisiana. This agreement including Appendices A & B, constitutes the entire understanding of the parties concerning the subject matter hereof, and shall not be modified except by a written agreement executed by both parties hereto.

IN WITNESS WHEREOF, the parties hereto, referred to herein as Publisher and Author, have executed this agreement as of the day and year first set forth.

_____   _____   _____   _____
    Publisher   DATE   Author   DATE

APPENDIX A

      Author hereby agrees to deliver the completed work ("Work") and to make the listed additions and/or revisions to the Work, which additions and/or revisions shall be delivered with the completed Work, on or before the ____ day of _____, 19__:

      Additions and Revisions:

_____   _____   _____   _____
PUBLISHER   DATE   AUTHOR   DATE

APPENDIX B

      In further considerations of the mutual rights and obliga-
tions of the foregoing agreement, Author and Publisher agree as
follows:

1. The Royalty to be paid to Author shall be _____%.

2. The Royalty advance to Author shall be $_____.

_____   _____   _____   _____
  PUBLISHER   DATE   AUTHOR   DATE

INDEX